Tips & Clips

Seasons and Weather

by Marilynn G. Barr

Publisher: Roberta Suid
Copy Editor: Carol Whiteley
Cover Design: David Hale

Call our toll-free number: 1-800-255-6049
E-mail us at: MMBooks@aol.com
Visit our Web site:
http://www.mondaymorningbooks.com

Monday Morning is a registered trademark of
Monday Morning Books, Inc.

ISBN 1-57612-144-5

Printed in the United States of America
9 8 7 6 5 4 3 2 1

Contents

Introduction

The interesting facts and creative craft projects in this book invite children to learn about the seasons and weather.

Weather Station Earth

Children will enjoy spending time in a reading and creative-play weather station made from a refrigerator box. Provide materials for children to make headbands, wacky weather vanes, bookmarks, weather calendars, and weather dolls. Ask children to help you set up the weather station and display weather charts for an inviting weather station center.

Weather

Share facts about clouds, rain, rainbows, snow, and storms. Then prepare a workstation for children to make cloud and rainbow creatures, place mats, rain sticks, sparkling raindrops, headbands, plastic storage bag snow globes, tornado bottle art, hurricane painting boxes, and a paper snowflake collection.

The Seasons

Discuss the sights, sounds, scents, and tastes of the seasons. Then provide children with materials to make headbands, wind chimes, and treasure boxes for each season.

Fall

Take children on a nature walk to collect colorful fallen leaves for a colors-of-fall leaf scrapbook. Use plastic grocery bags and mismatched mittens to make the sound of leaves swaying in the wind. Decorate your room with colorful falling leaves mobiles. Then make and share tasty ready-to-bake cinnamon biscuit bows.

Winter

Make a snowflake checkers game. Mimic the sound of crunching snow with a bread bag filled with packing peanuts. Decorate multicolored candy canes. Then help children create yummy giant gingerbread buttons laced with red licorice laces.

Spring

Children will enjoy making the sounds of a spring storm with thunder boards, sticks, and clappers. Encourage them to use their imaginations to create freestanding kite sculptures and pasta flower art. Then provide strawberries, and lots of mini marshmallows for children to form edible flowers.

Summer

Provide children with materials and patterns to make paper seashell collections. Transform small plastic drink bottles into sand castle bowling pins for a game of sand castle bowling. Listen to the sounds of the ocean through decorative sound tubes. Make refreshing lemonade ice cube pops while you share summer facts.

Seasonal Holidays

Discuss seasonal weather changes and holidays that occur during each season. Then provide children with supplies to make ship pockets and turkey baskets for fall; jingle bell gloves, giant kinaras, and masks for winter; glitter egg gardens and pasta star mosaics for spring; maple leaf sponge art and eyedropper bow ties for summer; and more.

Weather Station Earth Materials Request Form

Copy, fill in, and reproduce a request form for each child to take home.

Weather Station Earth Materials Request Form

Our class will be making a Weather Station Earth Center.
Please send the checked items to school with your child.

Due date: _____

Teacher: _____ Room: _____

Please fill in and return this form if you can volunteer.

Name: _____

Telephone: _____ Best time to call: _____

Materials List

- [ ] aluminum foil
- [ ] aluminum pie tins (small and large)
- [ ] bottle caps
- [ ] box (large enough to fit over head)
- [ ] buttons
- [ ] cellophane tape
- [ ] cellophane wrap
- [ ] crayons
- [ ] gift wrap tubes
- [ ] glitter
- [ ] glue
- [ ] jar lids
- [ ] margarine tubs and lids
- [ ] markers
- [ ] masking tape
- [ ] packing tape

- [ ] paper plates
- [ ] paper towel tubes
- [ ] plastic bottles
- [ ] plastic cups
- [ ] plastic milk containers
- [ ] refrigerator box
- [ ] scissors
- [ ] spools
- [ ] yarn

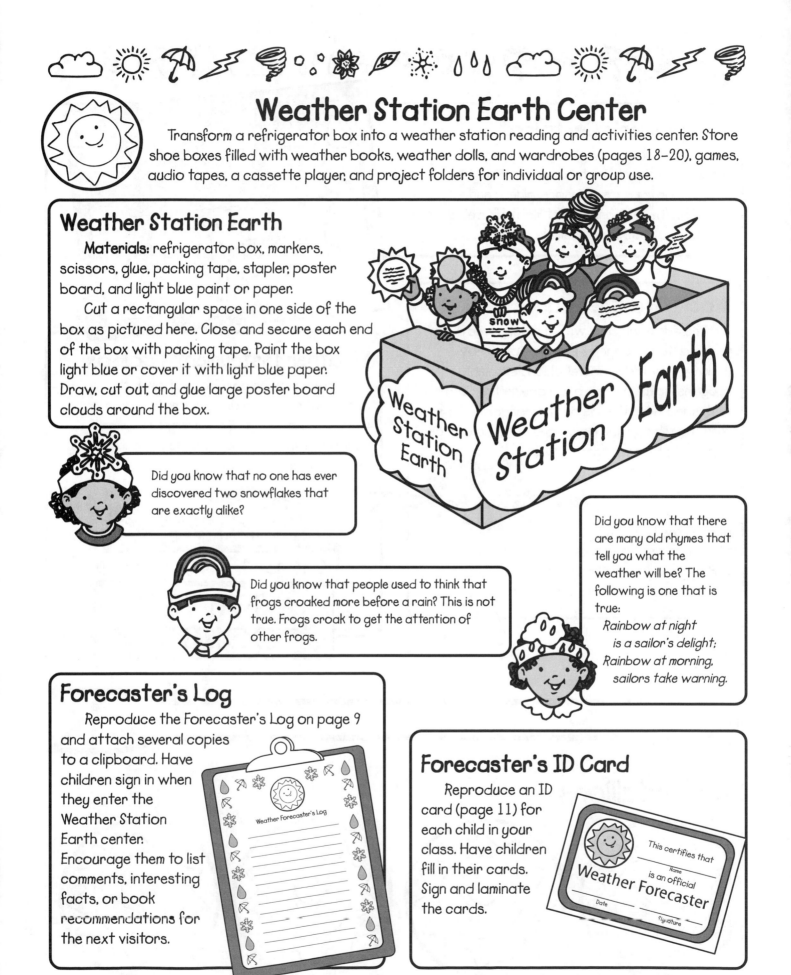

Weather Station Earth Center

Transform a refrigerator box into a weather station reading and activities center. Store shoe boxes filled with weather books, weather dolls, and wardrobes (pages 18–20), games, audio tapes, a cassette player, and project folders for individual or group use.

Weather Station Earth

Materials: refrigerator box, markers, scissors, glue, packing tape, stapler, poster board, and light blue paint or paper.

Cut a rectangular space in one side of the box as pictured here. Close and secure each end of the box with packing tape. Paint the box light blue or cover it with light blue paper. Draw, cut out, and glue large poster board clouds around the box.

Did you know that no one has ever discovered two snowflakes that are exactly alike?

Did you know that people used to think that frogs croaked more before a rain? This is not true. Frogs croak to get the attention of other frogs.

Did you know that there are many old rhymes that tell you what the weather will be? The following is one that is true:

Rainbow at night
is a sailor's delight;
Rainbow at morning,
sailors take warning.

Forecaster's Log

Reproduce the Forecaster's Log on page 9 and attach several copies to a clipboard. Have children sign in when they enter the Weather Station Earth center. Encourage them to list comments, interesting facts, or book recommendations for the next visitors.

Forecaster's ID Card

Reproduce an ID card (page 11) for each child in your class. Have children fill in their cards. Sign and laminate the cards.

This certifies that
_____
Name
is an official
Weather Forecaster
Date _____ Signature _____

Forecaster's Certificate

Reward children with a Junior Weather Forecaster's certificate (page 10). Provide crayons or markers, scissors, glue, a sun medallion (below), and a certificate for each child to color, cut out, and assemble.

This is to certify that
_____
Name
is an official member of the
Junior Weather Forecasters' Club
_____   _____
Date   Signature

Wacky Weather Vanes

Provide each child with a wacky weather vane patterns (page 13), an oaktag arrow (below), a wooden dowel, glue, a stapler, crayons, scissors, and a margarine tub filled with sand. Glue the lids on the margarine tubs. Turn the tubs upside down and cut a hole large enough to fit a wooden dowel. Children color, cut out, and staple or glue a wacky weather vane and arrow pattern to the dowel as shown. Push the other end of each dowel through the hole in the bottom of the margarine tub.

Weather Instrument Toolbox

Cover an open cardboard box with construction paper and decorate it with weather symbols. Add a variety of real and handmade weather instruments for children to use during creative play.

Arrow

Sun Medallions

Forecaster's Log

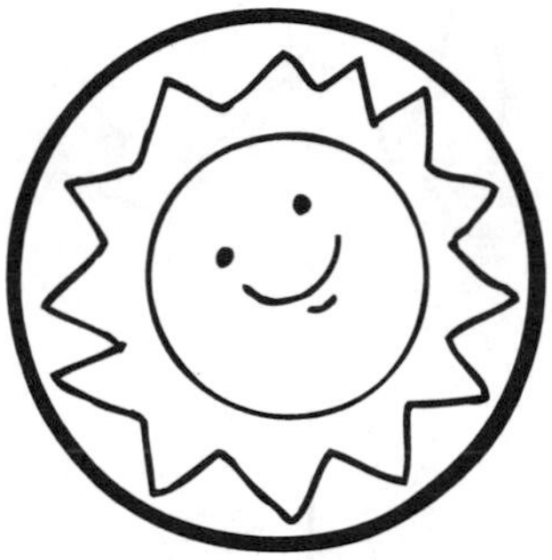

Weather Forecaster's Log

Certificate

This is to certify that

_____
Name

is an official member of the

Junior Weather Forecasters' Club

Attach Sun Medallion here.

_____
Signature

_____
Date

ID Cards

This certifies that
_____
Name
is an official
Weather Forecaster
_____   _____
Date   Signature

This certifies that
_____
Name
is an official
Weather Forecaster
_____   _____
Date   Signature

This certifies that
_____
Name
is an official
Weather Forecaster
_____   _____
Date   Signature

This certifies that
_____
Name
is an official
Weather Forecaster
_____   _____
Date   Signature

This certifies that
_____
Name
is an official
Weather Forecaster
_____   _____
Date   Signature

This certifies that
_____
Name
is an official
Weather Forecaster
_____   _____
Date   Signature

This certifies that
_____
Name
is an official
Weather Forecaster
_____   _____
Date   Signature

This certifies that
_____
Name
is an official
Weather Forecaster

Bookmarks

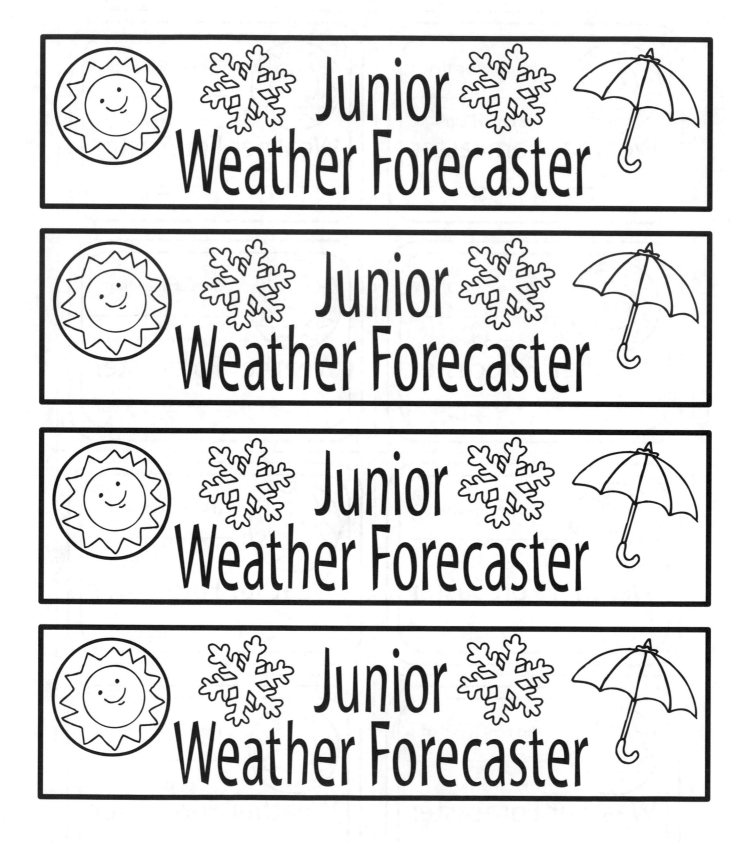

Wacky Weather Vane Patterns

Badger

Loggerhead Turtle

Platypus

Rhinoceros

Dolphin

Gorilla

Ostrich

Weasel

Weather Calendar

Make a large calendar to keep track of the weather. Enlarge, color, cut out, program, and glue the weather calendar on page 15 to a poster board. Make several copies and cut apart the calendar symbols (page 16). Attach a Velcro square to each space on the calendar and the back of each symbol card. Glue an envelope pocket to the bottom of the calendar to store the calendar symbols.

Barometers and Thermometers

Talk about the weather and how it changes. Explain that a thermometer is used to measure temperature and a barometer is used to help forecast the weather. Make a barometer and a thermometer (pages 16–17) to demonstrate how each works.

Barometer: Color and cut out the barometer patterns. Glue the barometer face to a paper plate. Punch a hole in the center of the barometer face and pointers. Use a brass fastener to attach the pointers to the plate. Demonstrate how the barometer needle moves from left to right as weather conditions change. In the morning, set one pointer to match the current weather. Later in the afternoon, move the second pointer to match your local weather station's report of barometric pressure. The space between the two arrows will show if the barometric pressure is rising or falling.

Thermometer: Copy and program a thermometer with either the Fahrenheit or Centigrade scale or both. Reproduce and laminate one for each child. Talk about the kinds of changes that occur when the temperature rises and falls. Use a wipe-off marker or crayon as you show how a thermometer works. Have children change the temperature on their thermometers as you discuss. Explain that Fahrenheit is used by most English-speaking countries and Centigrade is used for scientific work and by countries that use the metric system. Discuss the changes that occur when the temperature rises and falls.

Weather Wardrobes

Reproduce and provide each child with weather doll, wardrobe, and accessories patterns on pages 18–20 to color and cut out. Discuss different kinds of weather and how the weather affects what people wear. Have children dress their dolls with appropriate wardrobes as you introduce different weather conditions.

Weather Calendar Pattern

Sunday	Monday	Tuesday	Wednesday	Thursday	Friday	Saturday

Calendar Symbols

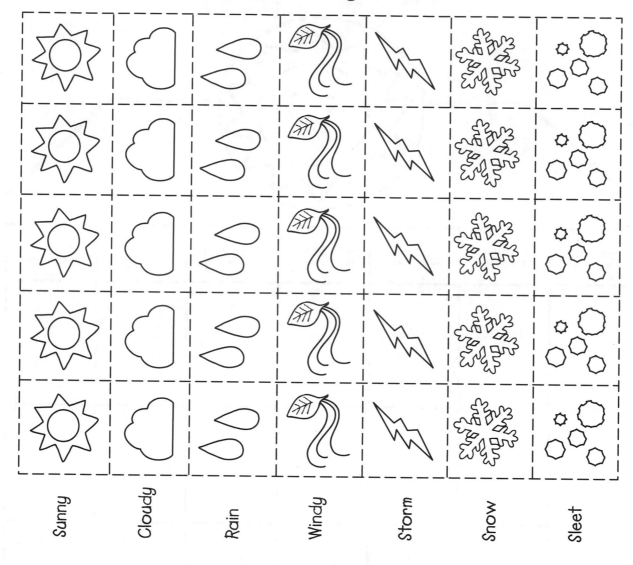

| Sunny | Cloudy | Rain | Windy | Storm | Snow | Sleet |

 Did you know that hailstones begin as tiny frozen raindrops?

 Did you know that sleet starts as very cold drops of water?

Thermometer Pattern

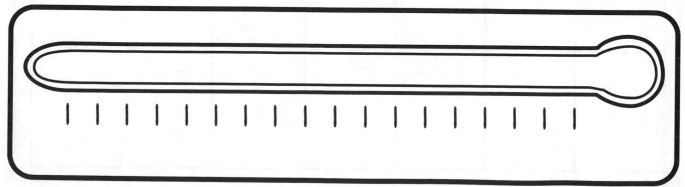

Barometer Patterns

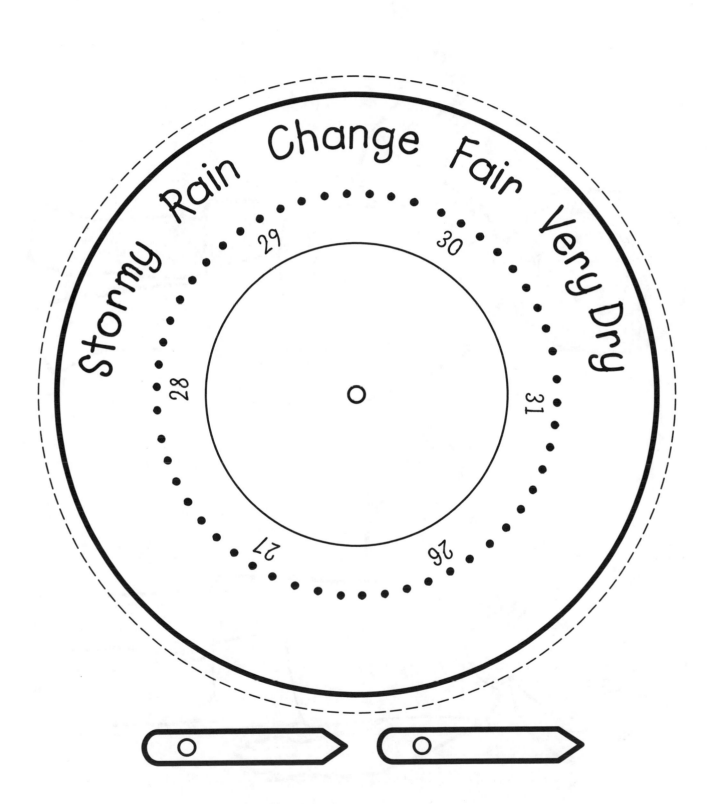

Weather Dolls

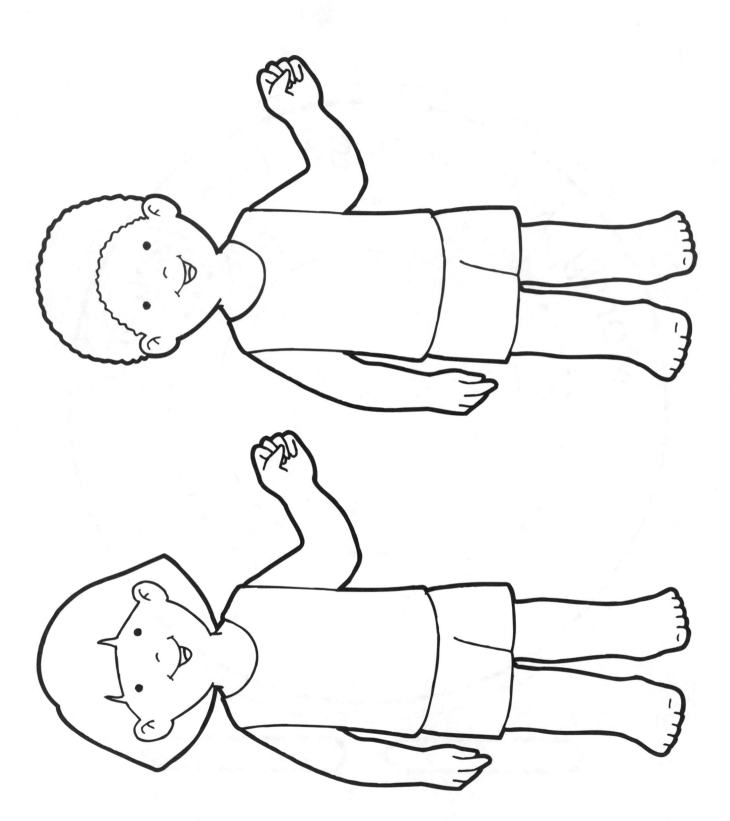

Rainy Weather Clothing

Cold Weather Clothing

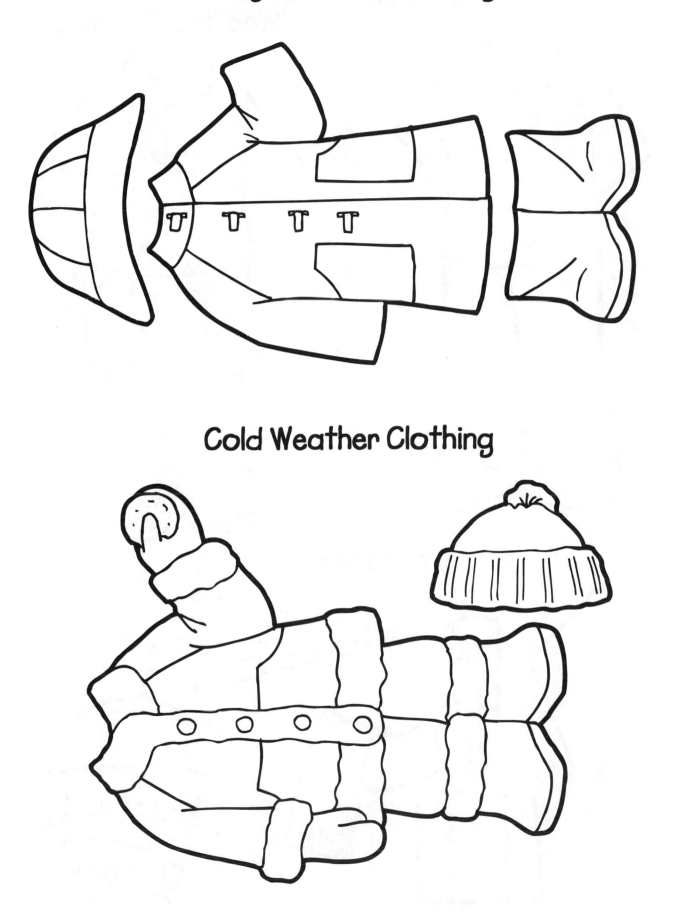

Cool Weather Clothing

Warm and Hot Weather Clothing

Accessories

Cloud Crafts Materials Request Form

Copy, fill in, and reproduce a request form for each child to take home.

- -

Cloud Crafts Materials Request Form

Our class will be making a variety of cloud crafts projects.
Please send the checked items to school with your child.

Due date: _____

Teacher: _____ Room: _____

Please fill in and return this form if you can volunteer.

Name: _____

Telephone: _____ Best time to call: _____

Materials List

☐ cans
☐ cellophane tape
☐ cotton balls
☐ crayons
☐ glitter
☐ glue
☐ hole punch
☐ markers
☐ oaktag
☐ paper plates
☐ scissors
☐ shallow containers for paint
☐ small boxes
☐ sponges cut into small pieces
☐ yarn

Clouds

Clouds are made up of tiny drops of water or ice crystals that float in the air. There are four types of clouds: *cirrus, stratus, cumulus,* and *nimbus. Cirrus* clouds are curly white clouds of ice crystals. *Stratus* clouds are thin clouds seen in the early morning or late evening. *Cumulus* clouds are large mountain-like clouds. *Nimbus* clouds are dark gray rain clouds.

Sponging Clouds

Prepare a workstation with light blue construction paper, shallow containers filled with white tempera paint, sponges cut into small pieces, scissors, crayons or markers, and glue. Demonstrate how to dip and sponge white clouds onto a sheet of construction paper. Show how to pat, twist, and drag the sponge to create a variety of cloud formations. Provide various items for children to cover with their sponged cloud art such as cans, or small lamp shades.

Cloud Place Mats

Have children sponge white clouds on light blue poster board clouds (page 23). Allow the cloud place mats to dry, then laminate them.

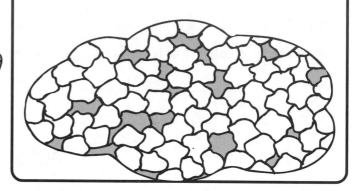

Did you know that a sudden heavy rainfall is called a cloudburst?

Cloud Creature Mobiles

Provide each child with cotton balls, scissors, glue, and his or her choice of a cloud creature (pages 24-25). Have children glue cotton balls to their creature patterns. When the glue has dried, punch a hole and lace and tie a length of yarn to each creature. Tie cloud creatures to wire clothes hangers for mobiles. Hang the mobiles in windows or open doorways or from the ceiling.

Cloud Pattern

Cloud Creature Patterns

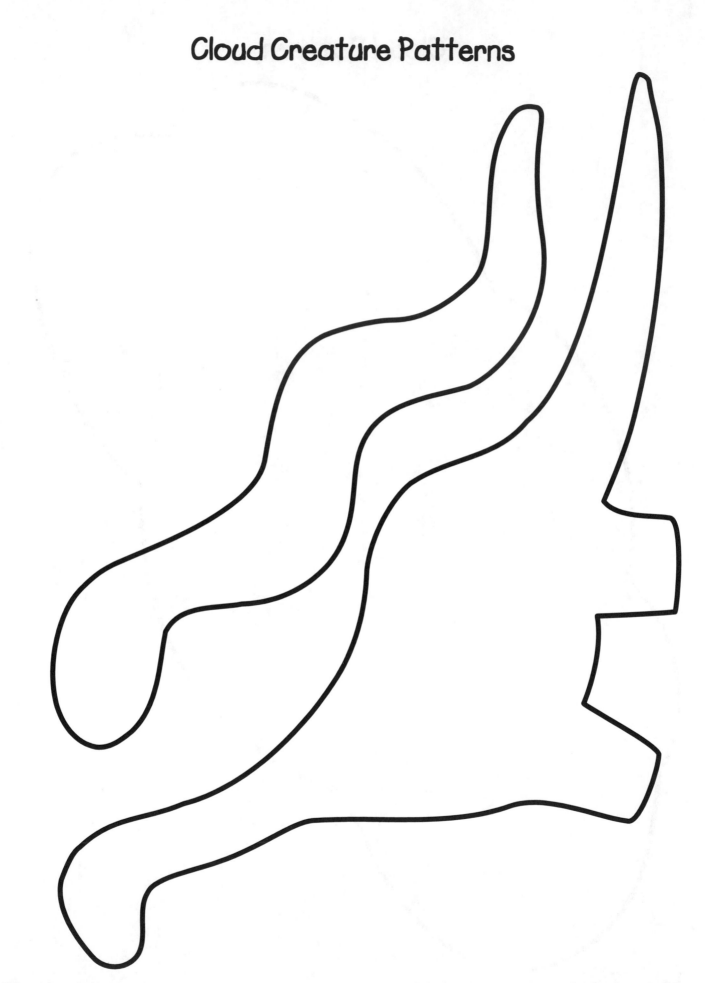

Cloud Creature Patterns

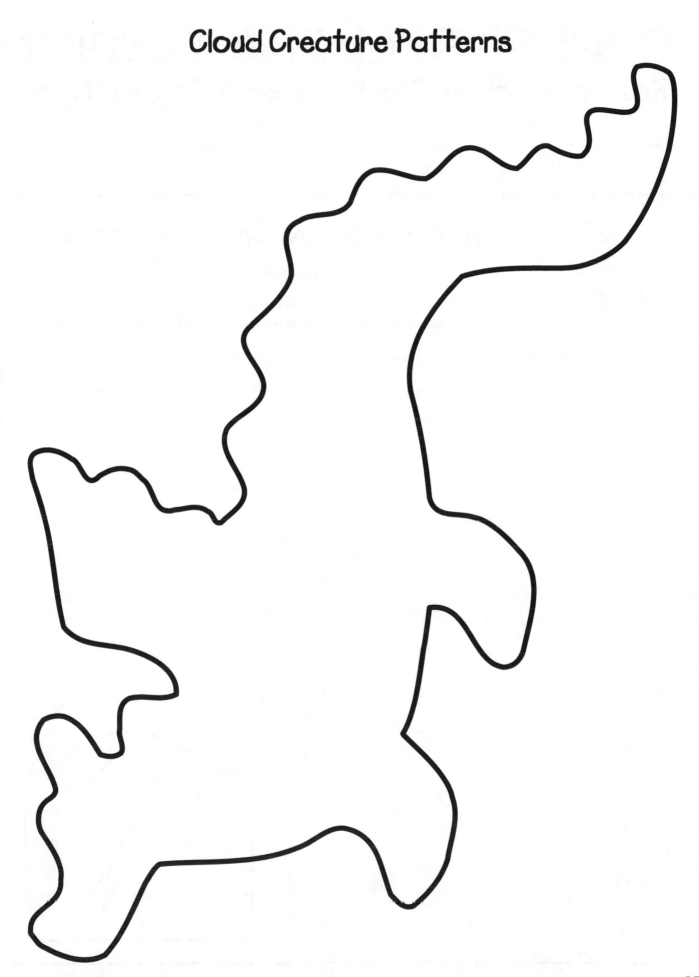

Rain and Rainbow Crafts Materials Request Form

Copy, fill in, and reproduce a request form for each child to take home.

Rain and Rainbow Crafts Materials Request Form

Our class will be making a variety of rain crafts projects.
Please send the checked items to school with your child.

Due date: _____

Teacher: _____ Room: _____

Please fill in and return this form if you can volunteer.

Name: _____

Telephone: _____ Best time to call: _____

Materials List

- [ ] aluminum foil
- [ ] beads
- [ ] beans
- [ ] buttons
- [ ] cellophane tape
- [ ] cotton balls
- [ ] crayons
- [ ] fishing line
- [ ] gift wrap tubes
- [ ] glitter
- [ ] glue
- [ ] macaroni

- [ ] margarine tubs and lids
- [ ] markers
- [ ] masking tape
- [ ] rice
- [ ] scissors
- [ ] sequins
- [ ] yarn

Rain

Rain is the moisture that is taken up into the air from the Earth. This process is called evaporation. The air that carries the moisture is warm. As the warm air rises it begins to cool and clouds form. Drops of water form in the clouds. Air continues to carry the drops of water upward until they become heavy and finally drop as raindrops.

Rain Brush

On a rainy day, provide children with art paper, paintbrushes, and paint. Have each child paint free-form designs on his or her paper. Then while they are still moist, place the paintings in the rain. Children will enjoy watching the raindrops create unusual designs as they mix with the paint.

Sparkling Raindrops

Prepare a workstation with oaktag raindrops (page 28), glue, paintbrushes, shallow containers, glitter, fishing line, and a hole punch. Pour glue into shallow containers. Show children how to paint a thin layer of glue on an oaktag raindrop, then sprinkle glitter over the glue. When the glue is dry, have children do the same to the opposite side of their raindrops. When the glue is dry, punch a hole and tie a length of fishing line to each raindrop. Hang raindrops from the ceiling.

The Sound of Rain

You will need a gift wrap tube, aluminum foil, crayons, scissors, rice, a margarine tub, and masking tape to make the sound of rain. Cover one end of the tube with masking tape. Tear a length of aluminum foil twice the length of the gift wrap tube. Crush and twist the foil into a spiral form that will fit inside the tube. Carefully slide the foil twist inside the tube. Then fill the margarine tub with rice and pour it inside the tube. Use masking tape to close the tube. Decorate the outside of the tube. Then cut and glue aluminum foil raindrops around the tube. Hold your rain stick upright for all the rice to fall to the bottom, then slowly turn the tube upside down. The rice falling against the foil will sound like raindrops.

I'm Singing in the Rain

Provide children with poster board, crayons, markers, scissors, glue, and oaktag rain boots and umbrellas (pages 28-29). Have each child draw a picture of himself or herself singing in the rain. Then have children color and glue the boots and umbrella to their drawings.

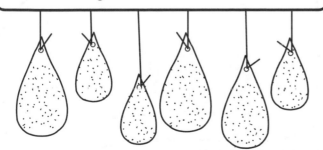

Raindrop Patterns

Rain Boot Patterns

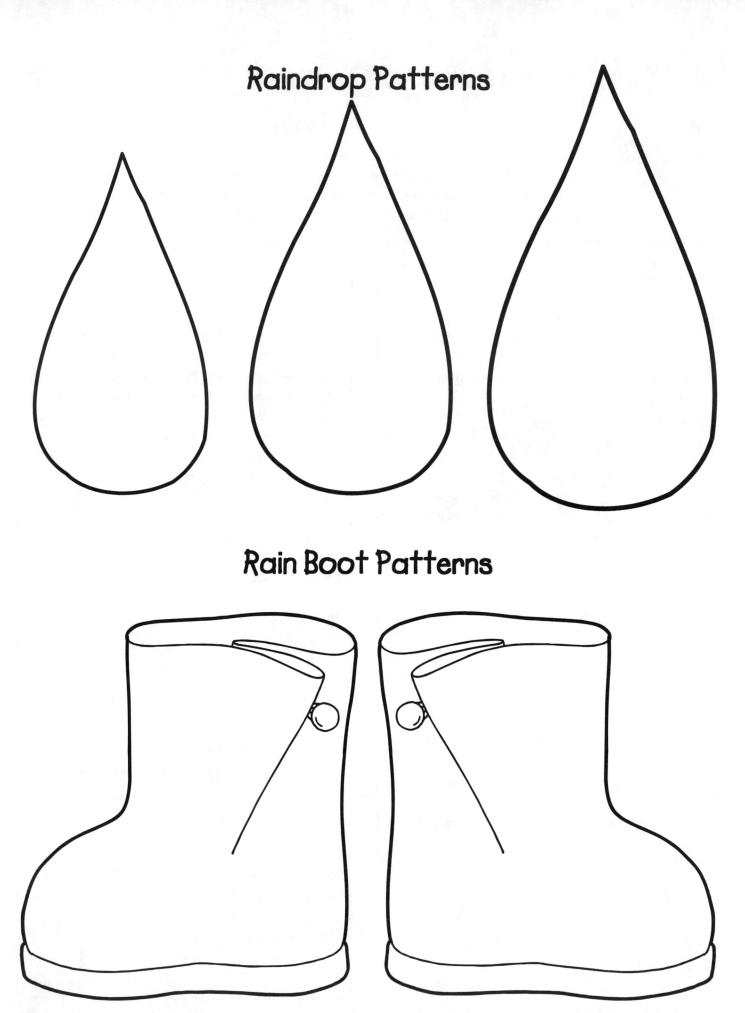

Umbrella Pattern

Rainbows

A rainbow is an arch of colors that appears when the sun shines after a rain shower. Seven colors are seen in a rainbow: red, orange, yellow, green, blue, indigo (a dark blue-black), and violet.

Rainbow Headband

Measure and cut an oaktag headband for each child. Provide crayons, markers, glitter, scissors, and glue for children to decorate their headbands. Reproduce the rainbow headband patterns on page 31 for each child to color, cut out, and glue to his or her headband. Fit the headband around each child's head and secure the ends with a staple or tape.

Over the Rainbow Frame

Children will need small photographs of themselves to complete this project. Provide oaktag patterns for children to make rainbow frames (page 31) and frame supports (below). Have children color and cut out the patterns. Help each child cut a picture window in the cloud pattern to fit his or her photograph. Position the photographs in the windows and secure with tape. Place the clouds over the rainbows and tape in place. Cut out and fold the frame supports as shown below. Then apply glue to each support tab and attach to the back of the assembled frames.

Rainbow Creatures

Reproduce the patterns on pages 32-33 for children to make rain creatures. Provide children with crayons, markers, colored construction paper, scissors, pipe cleaners, and glue. Have children color their rainbows using the traditional red, orange, yellow, green, blue, indigo, violet color pattern. You can substitute a navy blue marker or crayon for indigo. Then demonstrate how to color, cut out, and glue features to the rainbows to make a cat, dog, bunny, or pig.

Frame Supports

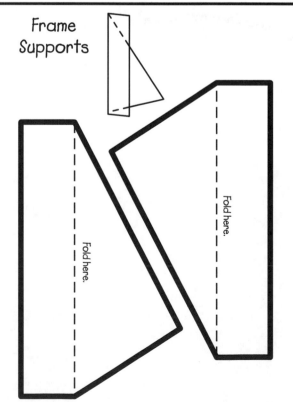

Fold here.

Fold here.

Rainbow Headband and Frame Patterns

Front

Back

Rainbow Creature Features

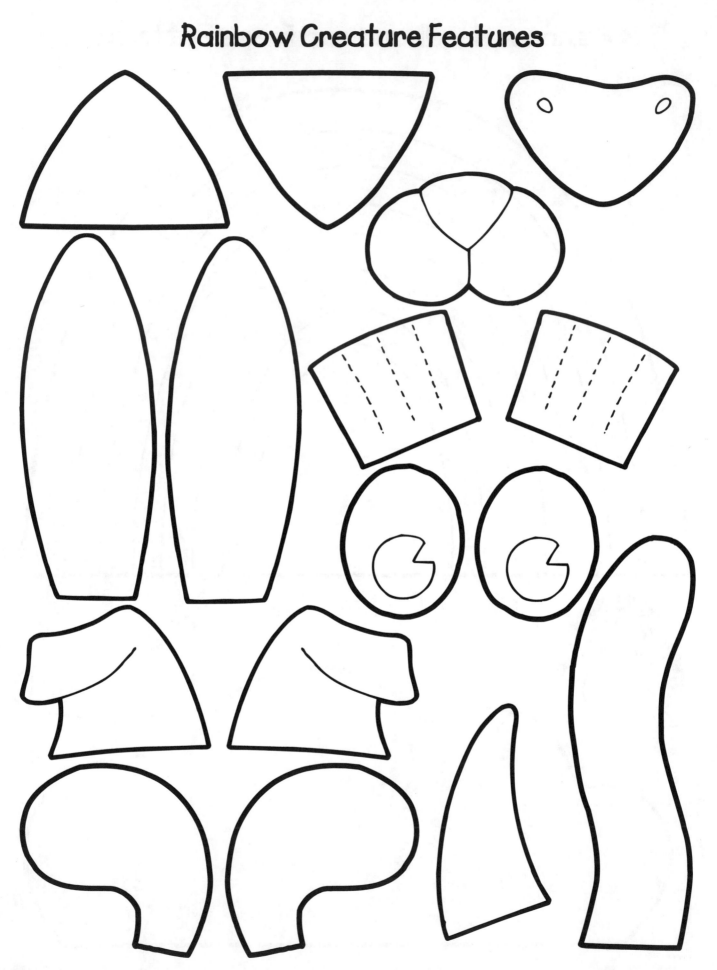

Rainbow Pattern

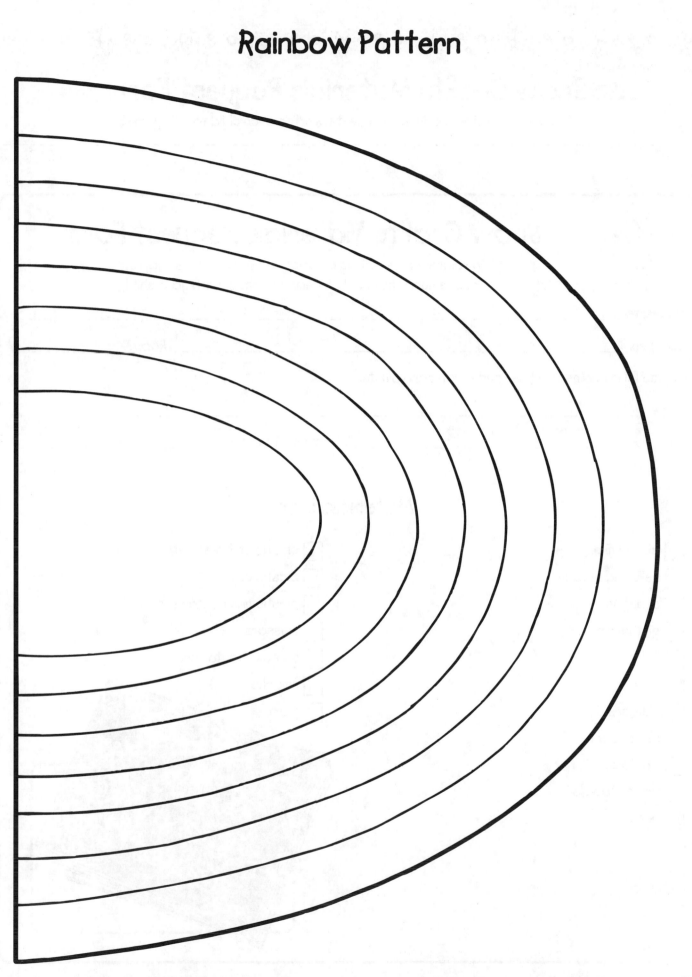

Snow Crafts Materials Request Form

Copy, fill in, and reproduce a request form for each child to take home.

Snow Crafts Materials Request Form

Our class will be making a variety of snow crafts projects.
Please send the checked items to school with your child.

Due date: _____

Teacher: _____ Room: _____

Please fill in and return this form if you can volunteer.

Name: _____

Telephone: _____ Best time to call: _____

Materials List

☐ aluminum pie tins	☐ plastic bottles
☐ cellophane tape	☐ plastic cups
☐ crayons	☐ plastic milk containers
☐ gift wrap	☐ scissors
☐ glitter	☐ shallow containers
☐ glue	☐ smocks
☐ markers	☐ yarn
☐ newspaper	
☐ oaktag	
☐ paper towels	
☐ pencils	

My Snowflake Collection

Snow

Snow is formed when the water vapor in clouds freezes into ice crystals or snowflakes. All snowflakes have six sides. Some are flat and some form long needles. The stud snowflake is rare. It is two hexagonal plates attached by a hexagonal column. The stud snowflake is formed in very cold temperatures.

Let It Snow! Let It Snow! Let It Snow!

Prepare a workstation covered with newspaper. Provide drawing paper, crayons, markers, white tempera paint, shallow containers or pie tins, old toothbrushes, and smocks for children to paint a snow picture. When children are finished with their drawings, pour a small amount of paint in pie tins. Show children how to dip their toothbrushes into the paint, then thumb spray the paint over their pictures.

Did you know that snow chains were invented in 1904 by Harry D. Weed of New York?

Stud Snowflake

Did you know that it snows more in the Grand Canyon than in Minneapolis, Minnesota?

My Snowflake Collection

Make oaktag snowflake templates using the patterns on page 37. Provide children with snowflake templates, construction paper, crayons, markers, scissors, glue, and a variety of paper such as craft tissue, gift wrap, newsprint, magazines, newspaper, and paper grocery bags to make snowflake collection scrapbooks. Have children decorate a construction paper cover. Stack and punch holes through the cover and several more sheets of construction paper. Lace and tie yarn through the holes to form books. Show children how to trace, cut out, and glue snowflakes from a variety of paper in their scrapbooks. Then have them write a name for each snowflake.

Snow Globe in a Bag

Children copy, color, cut out, and glue two snow globe patterns (page 36) back to back. They place their two-sided snow globe inside a resealable plastic bag. Fill a container with glitter and pour some into each bag. Press the bags flat while sealing.

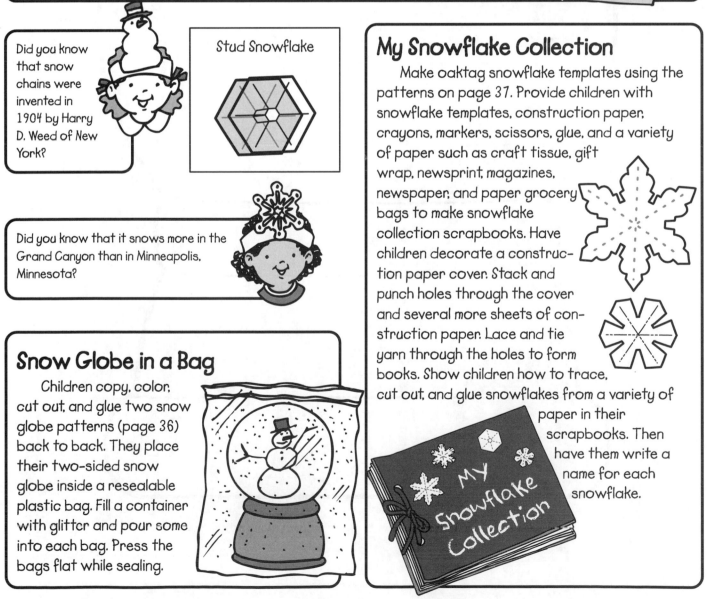

Snow Globe Pattern

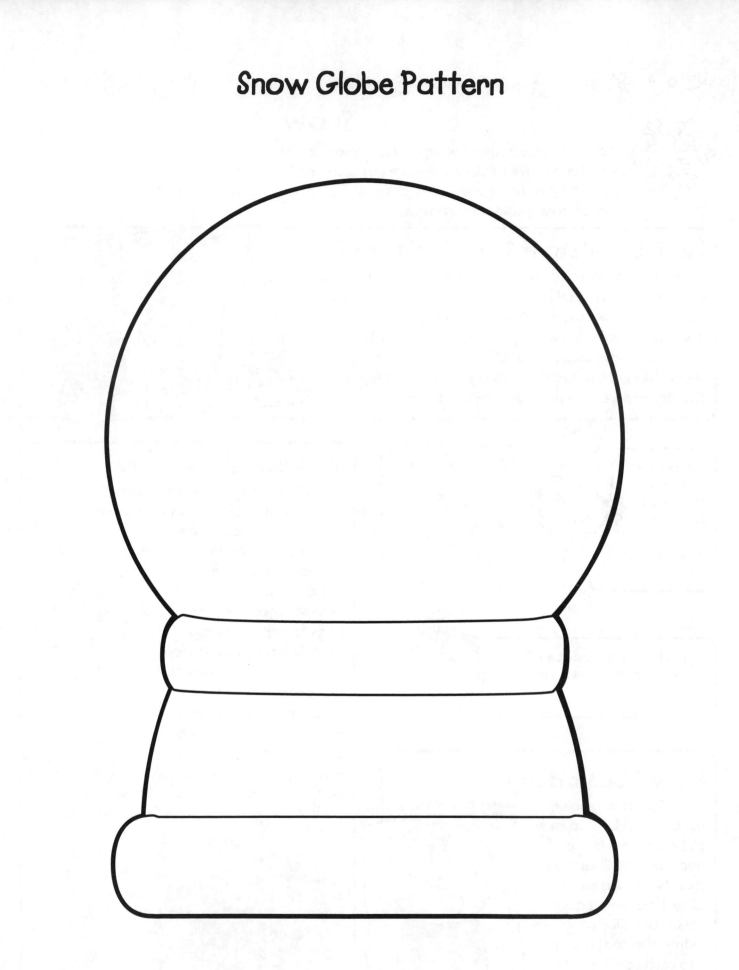

Snowflakes

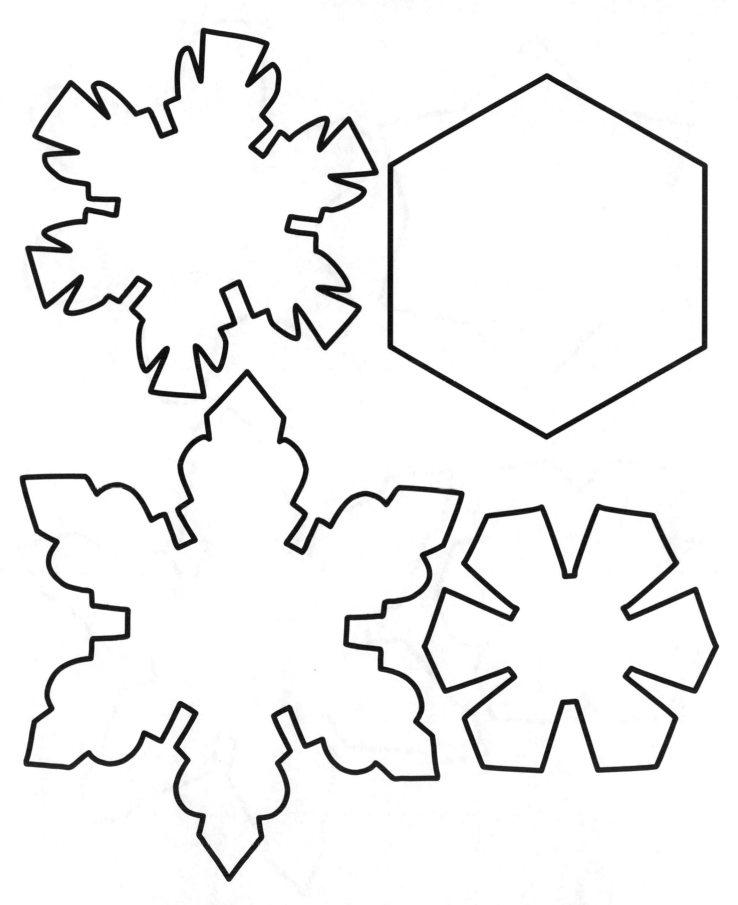

Snowflakes

Storm Crafts Materials Request Form

Copy, fill in, and reproduce a request form for each child to take home.

Storm Crafts Materials Request Form

Our class will be making a variety of storm crafts projects.
Please send the checked items to school with your child.

Due date: _____

Teacher: _____ Room: _____

Please fill in and return this form if you can volunteer.

Name: _____

Telephone: _____ Best time to call: _____

Materials List

- [ ] aluminum foil
- [ ] aluminum pie tins (small and large)
- [ ] beans
- [ ] buttons
- [ ] cellophane tape
- [ ] crayons
- [ ] glitter
- [ ] glue
- [ ] jar lids
- [ ] margarine tubs and lids
- [ ] markers
- [ ] masking tape
- [ ] packing tape
- [ ] paint

- [ ] paintbrushes
- [ ] pipe cleaners
- [ ] plastic cups
- [ ] plastic drink bottles
- [ ] plastic storage box with lid
- [ ] scissors
- [ ] yarn

Storms

Storms are caused by the differences in temperature, pressure, and moisture in the air. Storms can include one or more of the following: strong winds, rain, snow, hail, thunder, or lightning. Hurricanes are whirling storms with strong winds that form over the ocean.

Storm Headbands

Measure and cut an oaktag headband for each child. Provide crayons, markers, glitter, scissors, and glue for children to decorate their headbands. Reproduce weather patterns (pages 31, 41, 42) for each child to color, cut out, and glue to his or her headband. Cut foil raindrops to add to cloud headbands. Fit the headband around each child's head and secure the ends with a staple or tape.

Naming Hurricanes

Hurricanes were once named for religious figures. In the 1940s, hurricanes were named for the wives and girlfriends of soldiers. In 1953, the National Weather Service started naming hurricanes after women in alphabetical order. Today, hurricanes are named after both women and men. The letters Q, U, X, Y, and Z are not used. Invite children to help you write a list of names you might use to name local storms.

Did you know that the water in raindrops travels from the ground to the air over and over again? When it goes up into the air it is called evaporation. When it falls to the ground it is raining.

Did you know that snow falls on about one third of the Earth's surface?

blank paper

Hurricane Painting Box

You will need a plastic storage box with a lid large enough to fit a sheet of construction paper, paint, tape, cotton balls, beans, pipe cleaners, buttons, and glitter. Fill shallow containers with paint. Have children dip cotton balls and the other items listed above in the paint and place them inside the storage box. You may want to pour glitter in the storage box also. Place the lid on the box and have children shake the box in a circular motion. Remove the lid and allow the hurricane painting to dry.

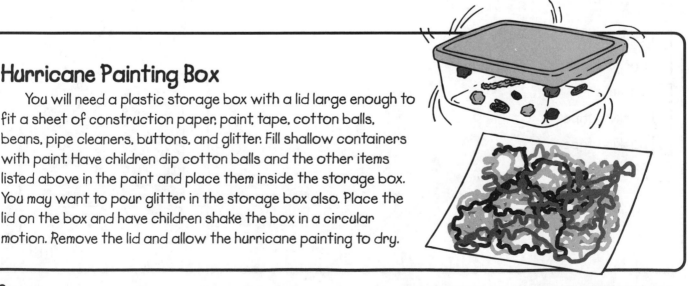

Lightning and Thunder

Lightning is the flash of light that occurs when an electrical current travels between clouds and the Earth. Thunder is the sound that occurs after a flash of lightning. The sound comes when the air heated by the lightning bumps into cool air. Hail is round balls of ice that fall from clouds during thunderstorms.

Lightning Bolt Messages

Create an instant message board for children to share new information with their friends. Reproduce several oaktag lightning bolts and place them in a shoe box with a pencil or marker. Allow children to write a message on a lightning bolt and provide pushpins to display lightning bolts on a message board.

Lightning Bolt Pattern

You will need small and large pie tins, paint stirrers, old mittens, a stapler, glue, pushpins, a hole punch, scissors, and yarn to make the following thunder crafts.

Thunder Curtain

Punch one hole in several pie tins. Cut 8 to 10 lengths of yarn to hang in your doorway. Lace and tie a pie tin to one end of a length of yarn. Measure one hand width and tie a knot in the yarn. Lace and tie on another pie tin. Continue doing this until you have several pie tins attached to each length of yarn. Use pushpins to hang the pie tin strands in your doorway. Use packing or other strong tape for metal door jambs. Each time someone walks through the doorway, your thunder curtain will make noise.

Thunder Sticks

Use crayons or markers to decorate two paint stirrers. Staple a pie tin to one end of each stirrer. Clap the pie tins together to make thunder.

Clapping Thunder

Staple, from the inside, a pair of old mittens to two pie tins. Clap the pie tins together to make thunder.

Tornadoes

Tornadoes are twisting windstorms. They appear in the form of a narrow cloud called a *funnel.* A tornado does not travel in a straight path. It spins and skips across the earth. Sometimes it goes up into the clouds and then suddenly down to the ground. A tornado causes damage only when it touches the ground.

Tornado Bottle Art

Create colorful bottle art with a plastic drink bottle with a screw-on cap, enamel paint, cotton balls, and beans. Prepare a workstation covered with newspaper and provide smocks. Pour small amounts of enamel paint into shallow containers and provide two bowls, one filled with cotton balls and one with beans. Demonstrate how to dip cotton balls into paint and carefully drop them inside a plastic drink bottle. Then add a handful of beans. Screw the cap on the bottle and turn it upside down. Hold the bottle upside down and twirl it around fast. This will force the cotton balls and the beans to spin around and paint the inside of the bottle. Trace or copy, color, and cut out the tornado pattern below. Tape it to the top of your tornado bottle art.

Tornado Pattern

Did you know that clouds fly higher during the day than during the night?

Fall Crafts Materials Request Form

Copy, fill in, and reproduce a request form for each child to take home.

- -

Fall Crafts Materials Request Form

Our class will be making a variety of fall crafts.
Please send the checked items to school with your child.

Due date: _____

Teacher: _____ Room: _____

Please fill in and return this form if you can volunteer.

Name: _____

Telephone: _____ Best time to call: _____

Materials List

- ☐ biscuits (ready-to-bake)
- ☐ buttons
- ☐ cellophane tape
- ☐ cinnamon
- ☐ cookie sheet
- ☐ construction paper
- ☐ crayons
- ☐ fishing line
- ☐ glitter
- ☐ glue
- ☐ jar lids
- ☐ markers
- ☐ mittens
- ☐ old keys
- ☐ paper clips
- ☐ paper towel tubes
- ☐ pipe cleaners

- ☐ plastic grocery bags
- ☐ scissors
- ☐ shoe boxes
- ☐ small boxes
- ☐ stapler
- ☐ sugar
- ☐ wire hangers
- ☐ yarn

Fall

Autumn is the season of the year that comes between summer and winter. It is also called *fall* because it is the time of year when leaves fall from trees. In the Northern Hemisphere, fall begins on September 23. This day is called the *autumnal equinox*.

Fall Headbands

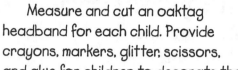

Measure and cut an oaktag headband for each child. Provide crayons, markers, glitter, scissors, and glue for children to decorate their headbands. Reproduce the fall patterns on pages 45-46 for each child to choose one to color, cut out, and glue to his or her headband. Fit the headband around each child's head and secure the ends with a staple or tape.

A Fall Treasure Box

Each child will need a shoe box, fall patterns (pages 45-46), crayons, markers, scissors, glue, construction paper, and other craft supplies such as glitter, yarn, buttons, pipe cleaners, seeds, beans, and macaroni to create fall treasure boxes. Help children write their names on their boxes.

Cinnamon Bows

You will need a can of ready-to-bake biscuits, cinnamon, sugar, a cookie sheet, a shallow bowl, and an adult helper. Preheat the oven as listed in the biscuit directions. Mix and stir cinnamon and sugar in a shallow bowl and set aside. Open and separate a can of biscuits. Then separate each biscuit into three equal portions. Press a biscuit portion in the cinnamon-sugar mixture. Stretch and twist the biscuit portion into the shape of a bow as shown. Gently press the bow into the cinnamon-sugar mixture again. Then place it on an ungreased cookie sheet. Repeat these steps for the rest of the biscuit portions. Follow the cooking time listed on the can of biscuits. When done, allow the biscuits to cool before eating.

Fall Wind Chimes

You will need 5 fall patterns (page 45-46), a hanger, yarn, a hammer, a large nail, 5 metal jar lids, 5 large buttons or old keys, crayons, markers, scissors, glue, and a hole punch, to make a fall wind chime. Bend the hanger to form a circle as shown. Color, cut out, and glue the fall patterns to the lids. Use a hammer and nail to punch a hole through each lid. Cut two matching lengths of yarn. Lace and tie one length to a lid and one to a key, paper clip, or button. Then tie each loose end to the hanger circle. Continue cutting two matching shorter or longer lengths to tie to the remaining lids and keys or buttons. Finish attaching all chime strands to the hanger circle. Then tie a length of yarn to the top of the hanger and hang from a tree, an open doorway, or the ceiling.

Fall Patterns

Fall Patterns

The Colors of Fall Leaf Scrapbook

Reproduce the scrapbook pages on 48-49 for each child. Provide construction paper, crayons, markers, yarn, buttons, scissors, glue, magazines, and a hole punch for children to make fall scrapbooks. Take children on a nature walk to collect fall leaves from different kinds of trees. Have children begin with matching leaves from one tree. Write the fall color of the leaf in the space provided. Then have children glue leaves to the top of the tree trunk and list leaf and tree facts on the same page. Encourage children to add same-color cut-out pictures and matching craft items such as yarn snips, buttons, and paper scraps.

Falling Leaves

Make several colored construction paper copies of the leaf patterns on pages 50 and 51. Provide scissors, a hole punch, and yarn for children to make a falling-leaves curtain. Have children cut out and punch a hole in each leaf. Have them tie a knot at the end of a length of yarn and lace the yarn through the hole in one leaf. Then tie a knot about one hand width from the leaf and add another leaf. Have them continue doing this until there are several leaves on each length of yarn. Hang the falling leaves from the ceiling.

Wind in the Leaves

You will need a plastic grocery bag and a pair of old or mismatched mittens, yarn, scissors, a needle, and thread. Smooth out a plastic grocery bag on a table. Cut off the bottom and the handles. Fold the bag in half and cut fringe along the open edges. Lace a length of yarn through the folded edge. Pull it tight and tie a knot in the yarn. Sew the knotted edge of the plastic fringe onto the end of a mitten. Repeat the same steps for the second mitten. To hear the sound of wind in the leaves, put on the mittens and wave and shake your hands.

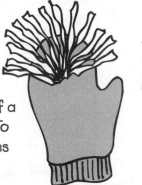

Fall Scrapbook Page

Tree Facts

Leaf Facts

Fall Scrapbook Page

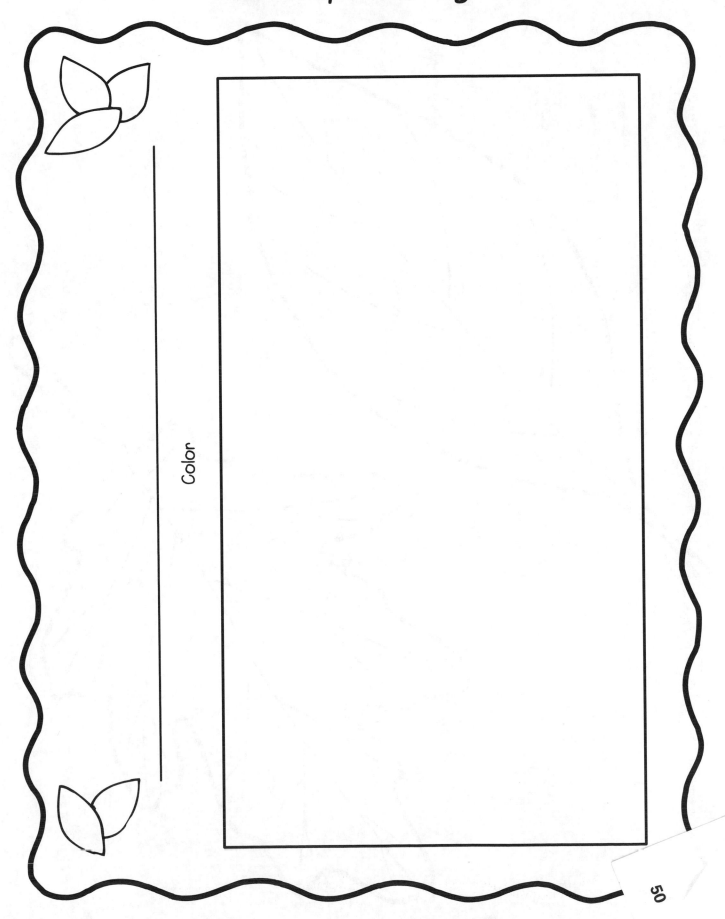

Color

Seasons and Weather © 2001 Monday Morning Books, Inc.

Fall Leaf Patterns

Fall Leaf Patterns

52

Winter Crafts Materials Request Form

Copy, fill in, and reproduce a request form for each child to take home.

- -

Winter Crafts Materials Request Form

Our class will be making a variety of winter crafts.
Please send the checked items to school with your child.

Due date: _____

Teacher: _____ Room: _____

Please fill in and return this form if you can volunteer.

Name: _____

Telephone: _____ Best time to call: _____

Materials List

- [ ] bread bags
- [ ] buttons
- [ ] candy canes
- [ ] cellophane tape
- [ ] cellophane wrap
- [ ] construction paper
- [ ] crayons
- [ ] fishing line
- [ ] gingerbread cookie recipe
- [ ] glitter
- [ ] glue
- [ ] grocery bags
- [ ] jar lids
- [ ] markers
- [ ] mittens
- [ ] old keys
- [ ] packing peanuts

- [ ] paper clips
- [ ] paper towel tubes
- [ ] pipe cleaners
- [ ] plastic grocery bags
- [ ] red licorice laces
- [ ] scissors
- [ ] shoe boxes
- [ ] small boxes
- [ ] stapler
- [ ] twist ties
- [ ] wire hangers
- [ ] yarn

Winter

Winter is the season of the year that comes between fall and spring. In the Northern Hemisphere, winter begins on December 21. This day is called the *winter solstice*.

Winter Headbands

Measure and cut an oaktag headband for each child. Provide crayons, markers, glitter, scissors, and glue for children to decorate their headbands. Reproduce the winter patterns on pages 54-55 for each child to choose one to color, cut out, and glue to his or her headband. Fit the headband around each child's head and secure the ends with a staple or tape.

A Winter Treasure Box

Each child will need a shoe box, winter patterns (pages 54-55), crayons, markers, scissors, glue, construction paper, and other craft supplies such as glitter, yarn, buttons, pipe cleaners, seeds, beans, and macaroni to create winter treasure boxes. Help children write their names on their boxes.

Candy Cane Reindeer

Provide a brown grocery bag reindeer (below) for each child to color and cut out. Help each child cut two slits at the bottom of the pattern to insert a candy cane.

Winter Wind Chimes

You will need 5 winter patterns (pages 54-55), a hanger, yarn, a hammer, a large nail, 5 metal jar lids, 5 large buttons or old keys, crayons, markers, scissors, glue, and a hole punch to make a winter wind chime. Bend the hanger to form a circle as shown. Color, cut out, and glue the winter patterns to the lids. Use a hammer and nail to punch a hole through each lid. Cut two matching lengths of yarn. Lace and tie one length to a lid and one to a key, paper clip, or button. Then tie each loose end to the hanger circle. Continue cutting two matching shorter or longer lengths to tie to the remaining lids and keys or buttons. Finish attaching all chime strands to the hanger circle. Then tie a length of yarn to the top of the hanger and hang from a tree, an open doorway, or the ceiling.

Winter Patterns

Winter Patterns

Crunchy Snow Mittens

You will need an empty bread bag, cellophane wrap, a pair of old mittens, scissors, glue, and a stapler. Cut palm-sized sheets of cellophane wrap and place them in the bread bag. Close the open end with a twist tie. Staple, from the inside, a pair of old mittens to the ends of the bread bag. Carefully put on the mittens. Open and close your hands slowly to make the sound of crunching snow.

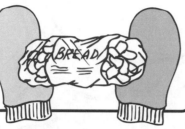

Gingerbread Buttons

Mix a batch of gingerbread cookie dough. Form large cookies and use a plastic straw to punch two holes in each cookie before baking. Bake according to the directions on the cookie dough packaging. Allow the cookies to cool. Provide each child with a red licorice lace. Then help the children lace and tie licorice bows through their buttons. (Note: If the holes close during baking, use a knife to carefully reopen them.)

Snowflake Checkers

Copy, color, cut out, and glue the snowflake checkerboard halves (pages 57-58) to a sheet of poster board. Copy and glue the snowflake checkers (page 59) to a sheet of poster board. Then cut the checkers apart. Have pairs of children play a game of checkers. Store the checkerboard and checkers in a large resealable plastic bag when not in use.

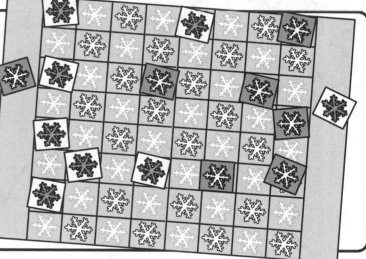

Did you know that the first artificial snow was produced in 1946 by Vincent J. Schaefer?

The Colors of Winter Candy Canes

Reproduce the candy cane and bow patterns on page 60 on white poster board. Provide crayons, markers, scissors, glue, and glitter for children to color their candy canes. Encourage children to think of interesting names for their color choices, such as Berry Red, Icy Blue, or Ivy Green. Help children write the name for each candy cane on a bow colored to match. Have children glue matching bows to their candy canes. Display finished candy canes on a "Colors of Winter" display board.

Snowflake Checkerboard

Snowflake Checkerboard

Snowflake Checkers

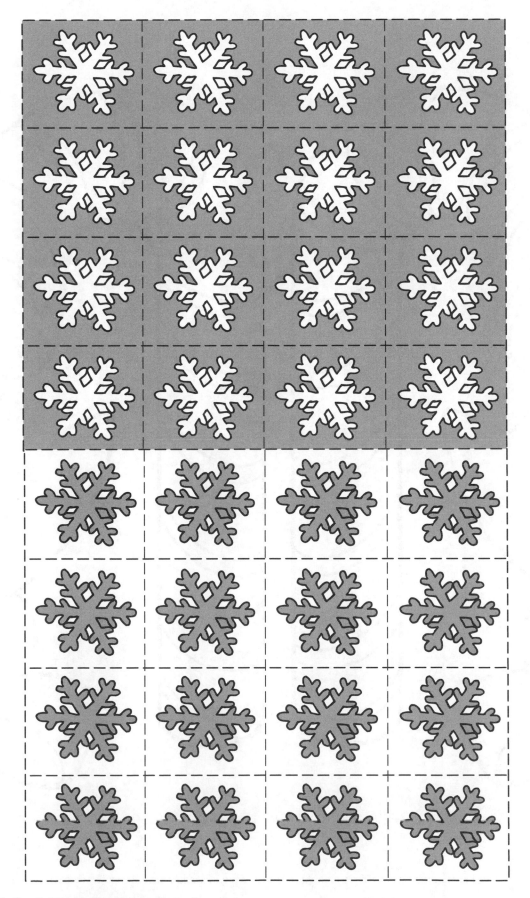

Candy Cane Patterns

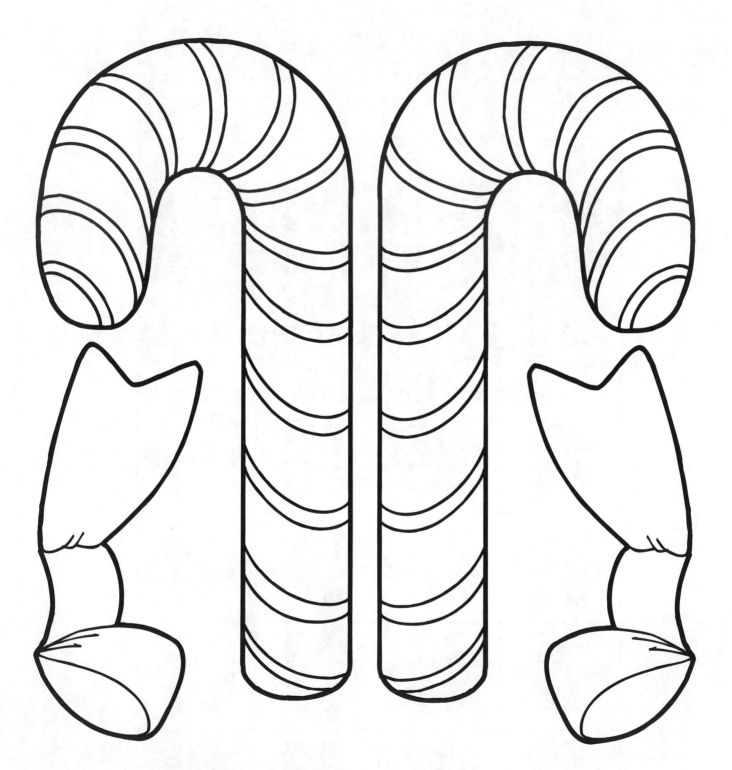

Spring Crafts Materials Request Form
Copy, fill in, and reproduce a request form for each child to take home.

Spring Crafts Materials Request Form

Our class will be making a variety of spring crafts.
Please send the checked items to school with your child.

Due date: _____

Teacher: _____ Room: _____

Please fill in and return this form if you can volunteer.

Name: _____

Telephone: _____ Best time to call: _____

Materials List

- ☐ buttons
- ☐ cellophane tape
- ☐ chalk
- ☐ crayons
- ☐ doilies
- ☐ gift wrap tubes
- ☐ glitter
- ☐ glue
- ☐ jar lids
- ☐ markers
- ☐ marshmallows
- ☐ paint stirrers
- ☐ paper clips
- ☐ paper plates

- ☐ pasta noodles (assorted)
- ☐ pipe cleaners
- ☐ plastic milk containers
- ☐ resealable plastic bags
- ☐ scissors
- ☐ small boxes
- ☐ vegetables
- ☐ yarn

Spring

Spring is the season of the year that comes between winter and summer. It is also the time of year when plants begin to grow again. In the Northern Hemisphere, spring begins on March 22. This day is called the *vernal equinox*.

Spring Headbands

Measure and cut an oaktag headband for each child. Provide crayons, markers, glitter, scissors, and glue for children to decorate their headbands. Reproduce the spring patterns on pages 63-64. Have each child choose one to color, cut out, and glue to his or her headband. Fit the headband around each child's head and secure the ends with a staple or tape.

A Spring Treasure Box

Each child will need a shoe box, spring patterns, crayons, markers, scissors, glue, construction paper, and other craft supplies such as glitter, yarn, buttons, pipe cleaners, seeds, beans, and macaroni to create spring treasure boxes. Help children write their names on their boxes.

Spring Wind Chimes

You will need 5 spring patterns (pages 63-64), a hanger, yarn, a hammer, a large nail, 5 metal jar lids, 5 large buttons or old keys, crayons, markers, scissors, glue, and a hole punch, to make a spring wind chime. Bend the hanger to form a circle as shown. Color, cut out, and glue the spring patterns to the lids. Use a hammer and nail to punch a hole through each lid. Cut two matching lengths of yarn. Lace and tie one length to a lid and one to a key, paper clip, or button. Then tie each loose end to the hanger circle. Continue cutting two matching shorter or longer lengths to tie to the remaining lids and keys or buttons. Finish attaching all chime strands to the hanger circle. Then tie a length of yarn to the top of the hanger and hang from a tree, an open doorway, or the ceiling.

Did you know that *mackerel* clouds are clouds that look like the scales on a fish?

Did you know that a rainbow can only be seen in the morning or late afternoon?

Spring Patterns

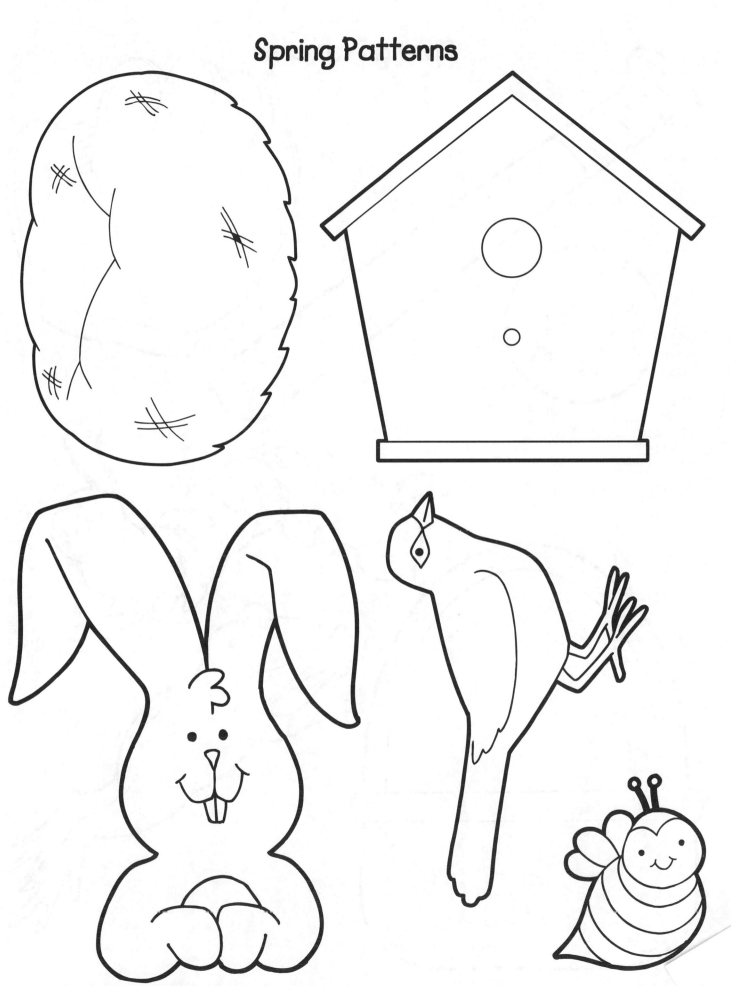

Spring Patterns

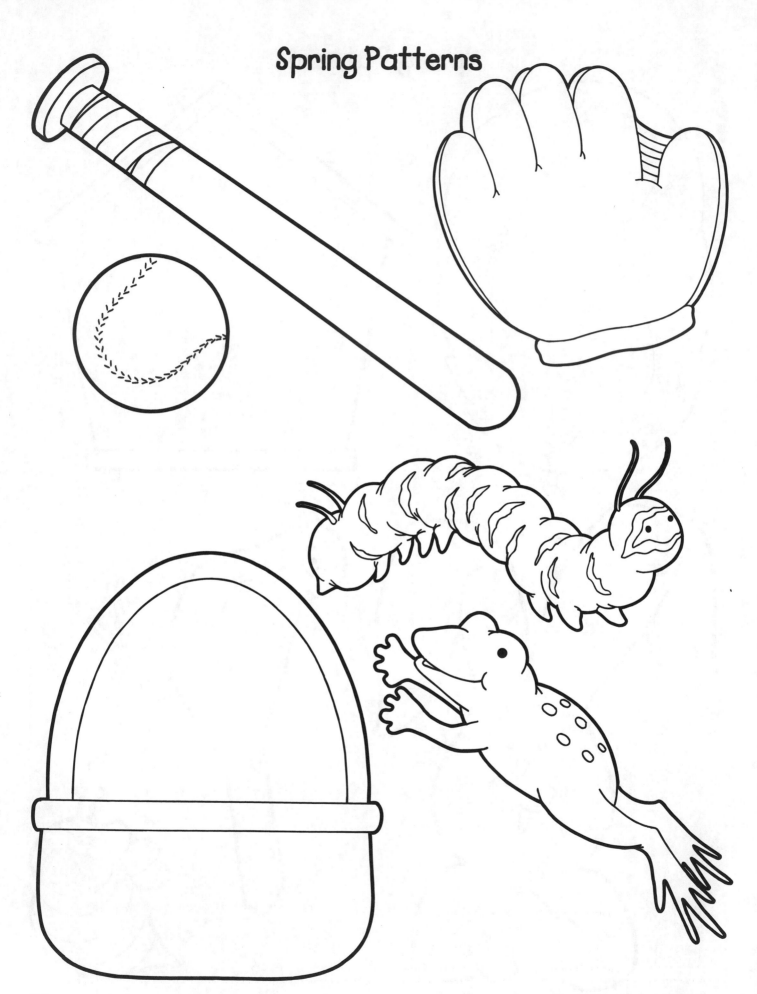

Thunder Boards

Cut a large sheet of dark poster board into long narrow strips. Provide children with white crayons or chalk to draw and color lightning bolts on their poster board strips. Demonstrate how to make sounds with a thunder board. Hold the narrow end of a poster board strip and rapidly shake it back and forth. This will make the poster board wiggle and make noise. You can also hold both ends of the board while rapidly shaking it up and down.

The Colors of Spring Pasta Flowers

Provide each child with a flower pot pattern and his or her flower choice (page 66). Place bowls of assorted pasta noodles on the table along with crayons, markers, scissors, glue, and construction paper. Have children color, cut out, and glue their flowers and pots on a sheet of construction paper. Then have them decorate their flowers with pasta. Mount finished pictures on a display board.

Seed Journal

You will need a variety of fruits and vegetables that contain seeds (see list below), construction paper, small resealable plastic bags, crayons, markers, scissors, and a stapler. Prepare a workstation covered with newspaper, smocks, a knife, and paper towels. Then provide each child with a seed journal form (page 67). Help each child open and staple the top back portion of a resealable plastic bag to his or her journal sheet.

Staple the back of bag to journal form

Then, working with one fruit or vegetable at a time, separate the seed or seeds while children watch. Share information about the seeds. Are the seeds edible? Do they need to be cooked before eating? Invite children to share their observations such as the size, color, shape, and number of seeds. Write the name of the fruit or vegetable on a paper towel and place the seeds on it to dry. When the seeds are dry, have children write the name of the seed at the top of their seed journal page. Then give each child a seed or seeds to place in the plastic bag. When children have several seed journal pages, have them make construction paper covers. Insert journal pages and staple.

Fruits and Vegetables List

Apples	Mangoes
Cantaloupes	Oranges
Cherries	Peaches
Cucumbers	Pomegranates
Grapefruits	Pumpkins
Green beans	Soybeans
Green peppers	Tomatoes

Flower Patterns

Seed Journal Form

Staple the back of a resealable plastic bag here.

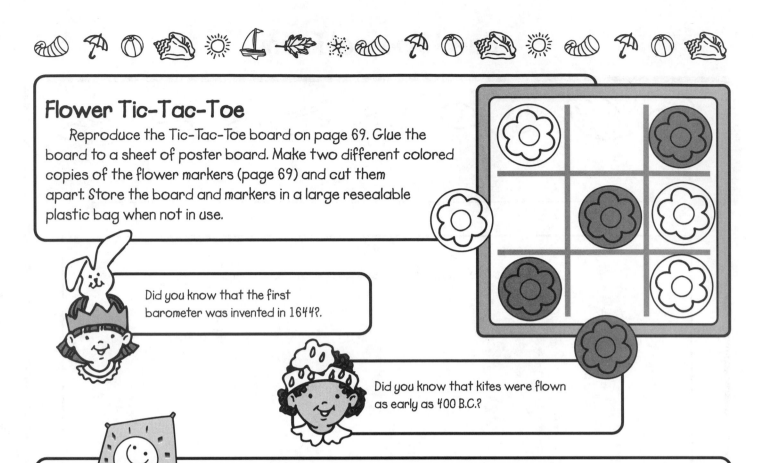

Flower Tic-Tac-Toe

Reproduce the Tic-Tac-Toe board on page 69. Glue the board to a sheet of poster board. Make two different colored copies of the flower markers (page 69) and cut them apart. Store the board and markers in a large resealable plastic bag when not in use.

Did you know that the first barometer was invented in 1644?

Did you know that kites were flown as early as 400 B.C.?

Joy of Spring Kite Sculptures

You will need a clean empty milk or juice carton, construction paper, a bag of dry plaster mix, a wooden dowel or paint stirrer, pipe cleaners, crayons, scissors, and glue. Provide each child with a kite pattern (page 70), three kite ties (this page), and a pipe cleaner. Make a batch of plaster. Then fill each child's carton with the plaster mix. Place a wooden dowel or paint stirrer in the carton when the plaster has stiffened. Have children decorate their cartons with construction paper. Then have them color, cut out, and glue their kite ties to a pipe cleaner, then to their kites. When the plaster has hardened, help children glue kites to the dowel or paint stirrer.

Kite Tie

Fruit and Marshmallow Flowers

Prepare a workstation with sliced strawberries, large marshmallows, and doilies. Have children wash their hands before they begin. Demonstrate how to create a flower pattern on a doily as shown here. Encourage children to use their imaginations as they design a fruit and marshmallow garden. Display finished designs for everyone to view before eating. (You may wish to substitute another type of fruit for children with specific allergies.)

Tic-Tac-Toe Board

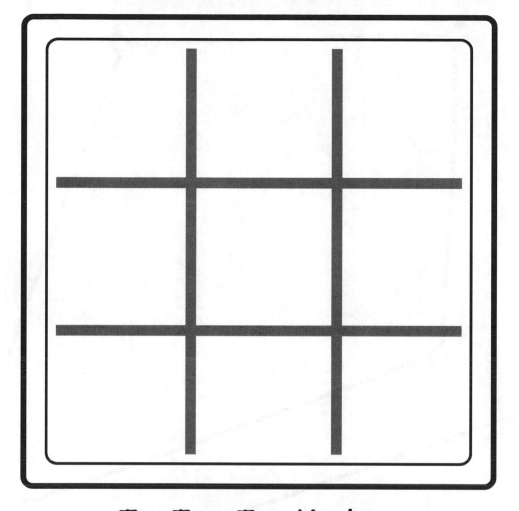

Tic-Tac-Toe Markers

Kite Patterns

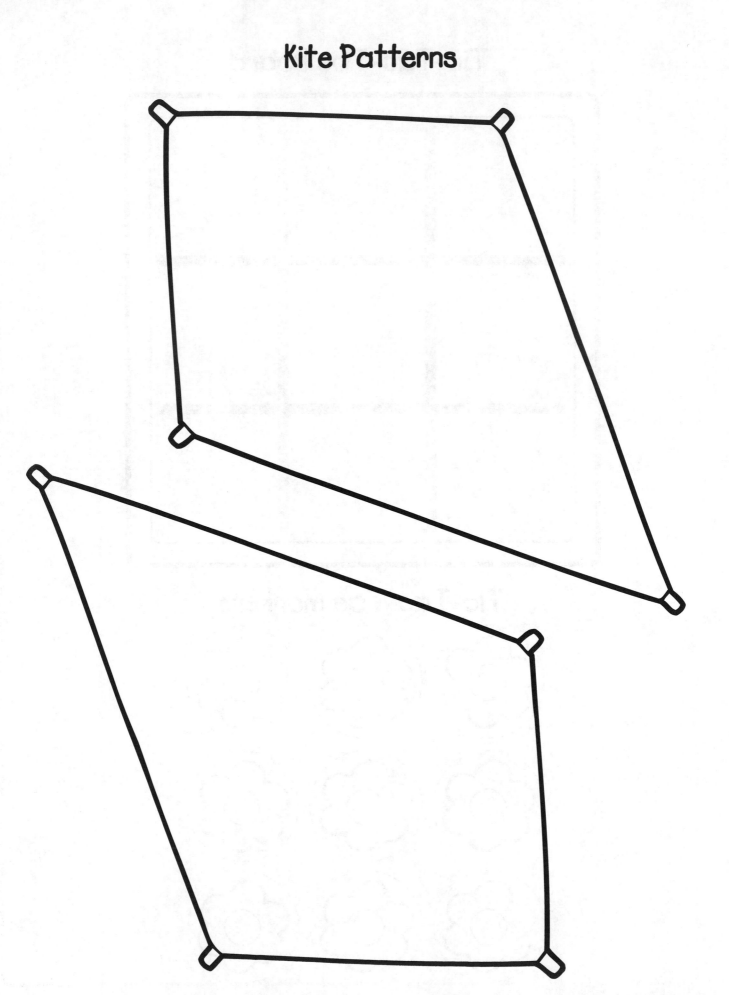

Summer Crafts Materials Request Form

Copy, fill in, and reproduce a request form for each child to take home.

Summer Crafts Materials Request Form

Our class will be making a variety of summer crafts.
Please send the checked items to school with your child.

Due date: _____

Teacher: _____ Room: _____

Please fill in and return this form if you can volunteer.

Name: _____

Telephone: _____ Best time to call: _____

Materials List

- ☐ aluminum foil
- ☐ buttons
- ☐ cellophane tape
- ☐ construction paper
- ☐ crayons
- ☐ gift wrap tubes
- ☐ glitter
- ☐ glue
- ☐ jar lids
- ☐ lemonade
- ☐ margarine tubs and lids
- ☐ markers
- ☐ masking tape
- ☐ old keys
- ☐ packing tape
- ☐ paper clips

- ☐ paper plates
- ☐ paper towel tubes
- ☐ plastic grocery bags
- ☐ sand
- ☐ sandpaper
- ☐ scissors
- ☐ wire hangers
- ☐ yarn

Summer

Summer is the season of the year that comes between spring and fall. In the Northern Hemisphere, summer begins on June 22. This day is called the *summer solstice*.

Summer Headbands

Measure and cut an oaktag headband for each child. Provide crayons, markers, glitter, scissors, and glue for children to decorate their headbands. Reproduce the summer patterns on pages 73-74. Have each child choose one to color, cut out, and glue to his or her headband. Fit the headband around each child's head and secure the ends with a staple or tape.

A Summer Treasure Box

Each child will need a shoe box, summer patterns (pages 73-74), crayons, markers, scissors, glue, construction paper, and other craft supplies such as glitter, yarn, buttons, pipe cleaners, seeds, beans, and macaroni to create summer treasure boxes. Help children write their names on their boxes.

Summer Wind Chimes

You will need 5 summer patterns (pages 73-74), a hanger, yarn, a hammer, a large nail, 5 metal jar lids, 5 large buttons or old keys, crayons, markers, scissors, glue, and a hole punch to make a summer wind chime. Bend the hanger to form a circle as shown. Color, cut out, and glue the summer patterns to the lids. Use a hammer and nail to punch a hole through each lid. Cut two matching lengths of yarn. Lace and tie one length to a lid and one to a key, paper clip, or button. Then tie each loose end to the hanger circle. Continue cutting two matching shorter or longer lengths to tie to the remaining lids and keys or buttons. Finish attaching all chime strands to the hanger circle. Then tie a length of yarn to the top of the hanger and hang from a tree, an open doorway, or the ceiling.

Lemonade Ice Pops

You will need a paper cup for each child, aluminum foil circles large enough to wrap around the opening of the cups, small plastic spoons, and lemonade. Fill each cup with lemonade. Carefully cut a slit in the center of each aluminum foil circle and insert a spoon. Place the foil-skirted spoons in the lemonade cups and secure the foil around the cup. Then place the cups in the freezer. When you are ready to enjoy your lemonade pops, remove the foil and place pops in a shallow pan of warm water to remove the cups.

Cut a slit in the foil to insert a spoon.

Summer Patterns

Summer Patterns

Sweeping Sand Mittens

You will need a pair of old mittens, fine-grit sandpaper, scissors, and a needle and thread or glue. Cut sandpaper circles and glue or sew to the palms of a pair of mittens. Put on the mittens and rub your palms back and forth to make the sound of sweeping sand.

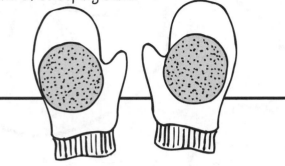

The Colors of Summer Seashell Collection

Provide each child with construction paper for a booklet cover, the shell patterns on page 76, and three seashell collection forms (page 77). Provide children with summer color crayons or markers to color their forms and seashells. Have children cut out the shells and glue them in the blank spaces on their forms. Help children write the shell names on their forms. Then have them decorate a construction paper cover and staple each child's booklet.

Sand Castle Bowling

You will need 10 paper towel tubes and sand castle wraps (page 79), small plastic grocery bags, shredded newspaper, a permanent marker, crayons, markers, scissors, cellophane tape, and glue. Color and cut out the sand castle wraps. Wrap and tape or glue a wrap around each paper towel tube. Stuff a small plastic grocery bag with shredded newspaper. Fold, tuck, and tape the bag to form a ball. Use a permanent marker to draw three dots on the ball to resemble a bowling ball. Assemble the sand castle pins in bowling formation (shown below). Then play a game of sand castle bowling with the children.

Bowling Formation

Did you know that bowling is one of the oldest indoor sports?

Seashell Patterns

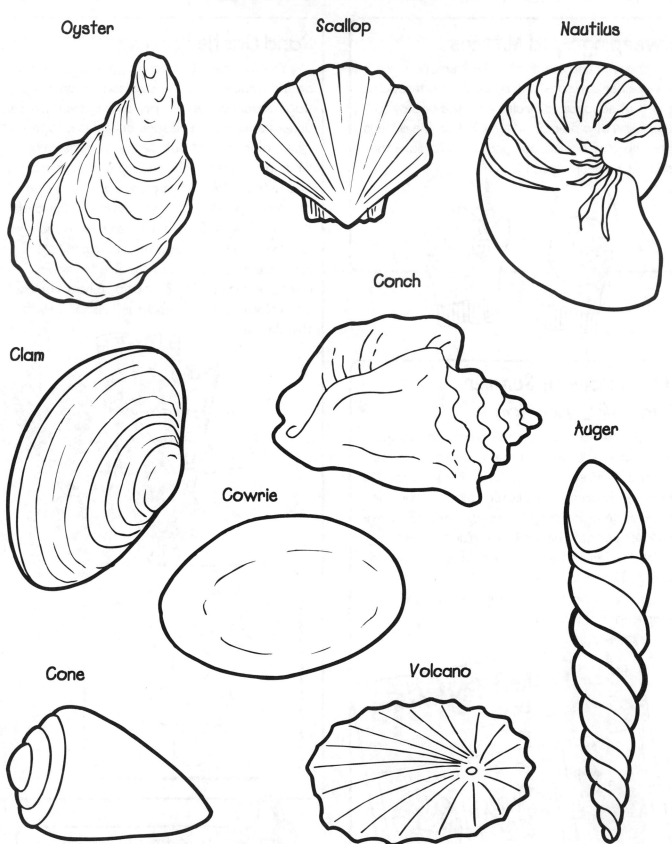

Oyster

Scallop

Nautilus

Conch

Clam

Cowrie

Auger

Cone

Volcano

My Seashell Collection

Name

Sounds of the Ocean

Provide children with paper towel tubes, the conch shell patterns below, construction paper, crayons, markers, and glue. Help each child cut a paper towel tube in half lengthwise. Have children wrap and tape construction paper around their tubes. Then have them color, cut out, and glue the conch shell patterns to either side of their tubes. Demonstrate how to hold a tube to your ear while covering the other end with your free hand in order to hear the sounds of the ocean. Make additional ocean tubes of different lengths from gift wrap tubes. Have children decorate the tubes with the seashell patterns on page 76.

Conch Patterns

Did you know that a breastbone from a goose was once used to forecast the weather?

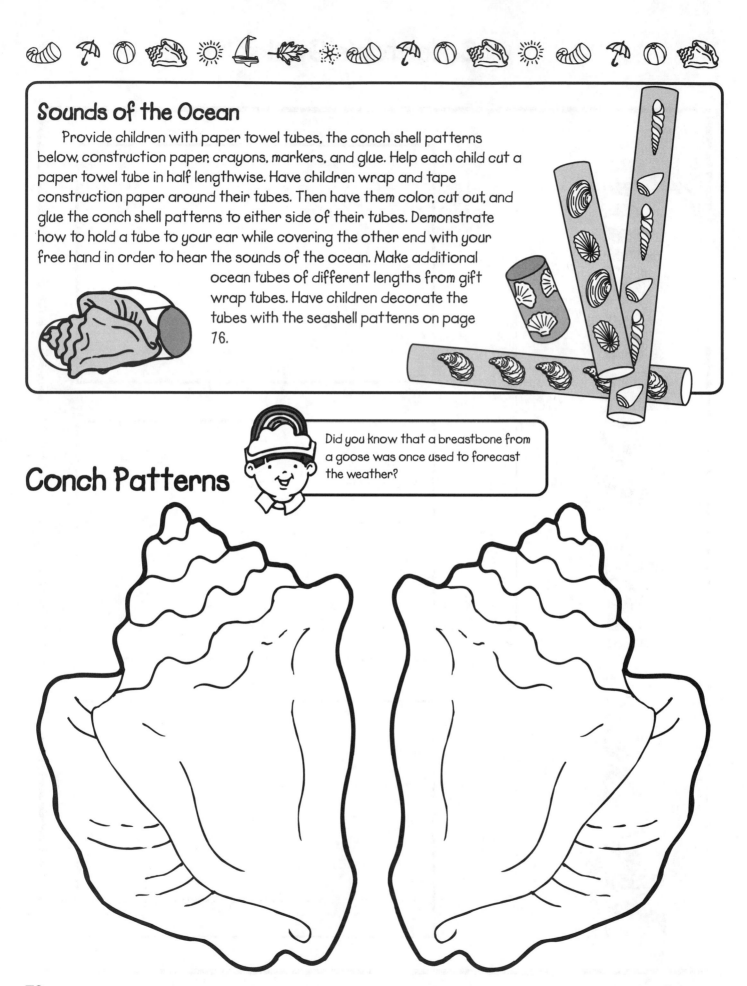

Sand Castle Wraps

Seasonal Holiday Crafts Materials Request Form

Copy, fill in, and reproduce a request form for each child to take home.

- -

Holiday Crafts Materials Request Form

Our class will be making holiday crafts.
Please send the checked items to school with your child.

Due date: _____

Teacher: _____ Room: _____

Please fill in and return this form if you can volunteer.

Name: _____

Telephone: _____ Best time to call: _____

Materials List

☐ aluminum foil	☐ paper plates
☐ beans	☐ paper towels
☐ buttons	☐ paper towel tubes
☐ cellophane tape	☐ pasta
☐ coffee cans with lids	☐ permanent markers
☐ craft tissue	☐ pipe cleaners
☐ crayons	☐ plastic bottles
☐ eyedroppers	☐ plastic grocery bags
☐ gift wrap	☐ plastic straws
☐ glitter	☐ pompons
☐ glue	☐ ribbon
☐ hole punch	☐ rice
☐ jar lids	☐ scissors
☐ jingle bells	☐ sponges
☐ markers	☐ stapler
☐ oaktag	☐ yarn
☐ old keys	

Seasonal Holidays

A holiday is a day when people take time out from work to celebrate a special event or person, such as Christmas, Hanukkah, Kwanzaa, Valentine's Day, and Martin Luther King Day. Each holiday has its own symbols, crafts, and activities.

Holiday Headbands

Measure and cut an oaktag headband for each child. Provide crayons, markers, glitter, scissors, and glue for children to decorate their headbands. Reproduce holiday appropriate seasonal patterns (pages 45-46, 54-55, 63-64, 73-74) for each child to choose one to color, cut out, and glue to his or her headband. Fit the headband around each child's head and secure the ends with a staple or tape.

Columbus Day

Many people celebrate Columbus Day in memory of the day, October 12, 1492, Christopher Columbus landed in the new world at *Guanahai*, which he renamed *El Salvador*.

Three Ship Pockets

You will need three small paper plates, paper plate halves, plastic drinking straws, a stapler, the patterns on page 82, crayons, markers, scissors, and glue. Color a large sun on the inside of one whole paper plate and clouds on the two remaining plates. Color and cut out the patterns. Cut two slits and insert a plastic straw in each sail, as shown on the pattern page. Secure the straws in place with tape. Staple each sail to a paper plate. Glue each ship to the bottom of a paper plate half and staple one to each paper plate to form a pocket. Mount the ships on a display board to use as note or message pockets.

Thanksgiving Day

Thanksgiving is a family holiday celebrated with a big dinner on the third Thursday in November. The first Thanksgivings were harvest festivals to give thanks for plentiful crops.

Grocery Bag Turkey Basket

Cut away the top portion of a brown grocery bag. Copy, color, and cut out one turkey head and two wings (page 83). Glue the head and wings to the bag. Make several colored construction paper feathers and attach them to the bag. Fill your turkey basket with holiday goodies. Or, use the turkey basket to hold holiday greeting cards to share with your children.

Ship and Sail Patterns

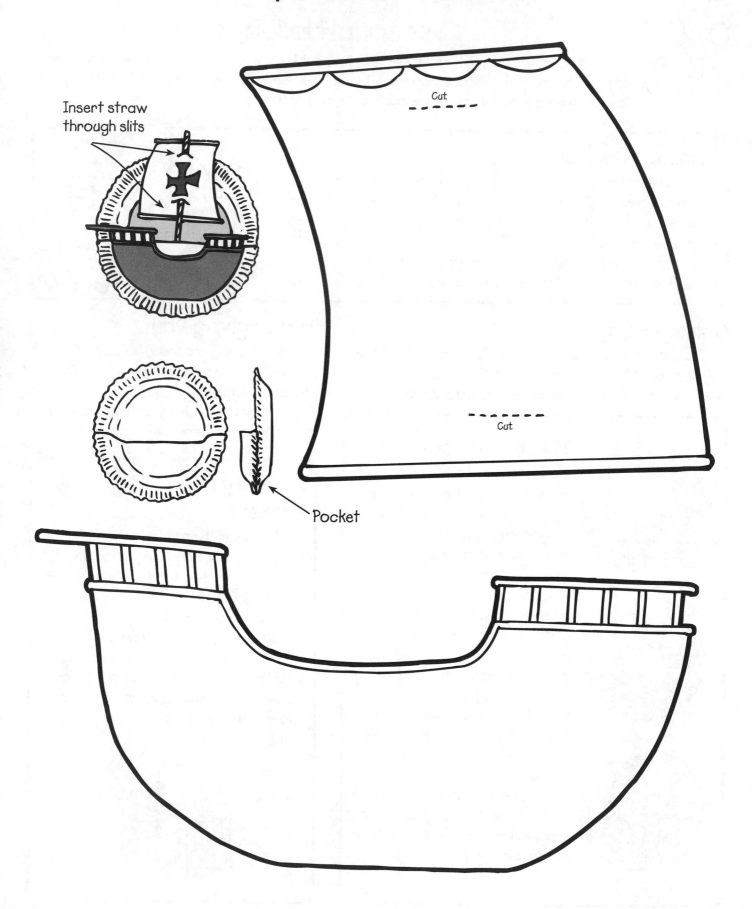

Insert straw through slits

Pocket

Cut.

Cut.

Feather Patterns

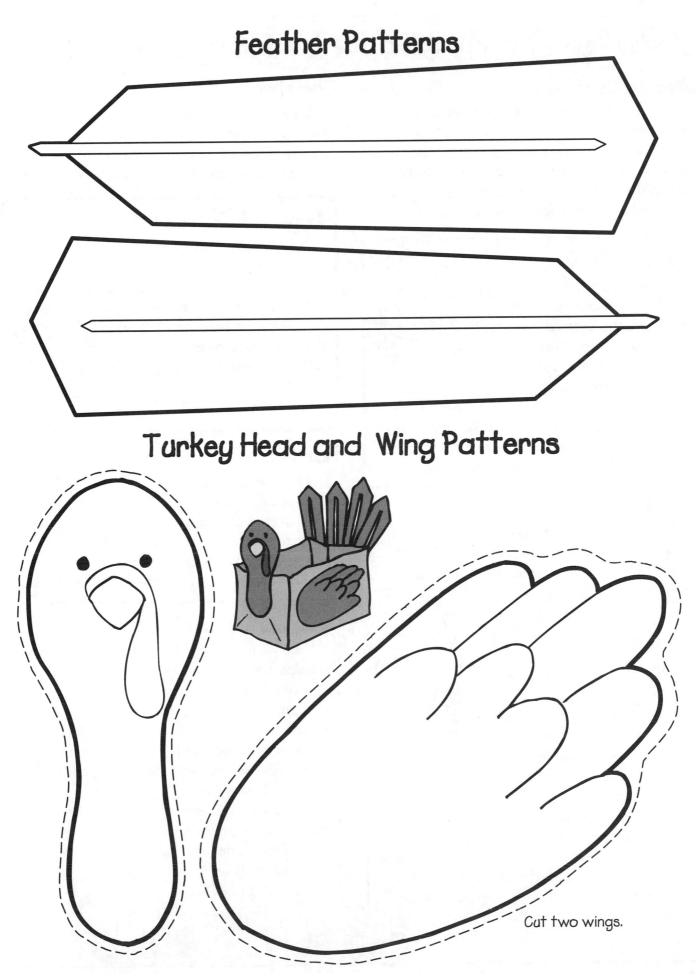

Turkey Head and Wing Patterns

Cut two wings.

Chinese New Year

Chinese New Year falls between late January and early February. Celebrations include festivals with dancing, stage plays, and arts and crafts booths. Each new year is represented by one of twelve animals: the boar, dog, dragon, horse, monkey, ox, rabbit, rat, rooster, sheep, snake, and tiger.

Dragon Shaker

Use crayons or markers, glue, and glitter to decorate the backs of two paper plates. Copy, color, and cut out two dragon patterns (page 86). Glue one dragon to the back of each plate. Place one of the plates on the table, dragon side down, and pour rice in the center. Place the remaining plate, dragon side up, on top and staple along the edges.

Diwali

Diwali is a winter holiday celebrated in India. Families prepare their homes and decorate with flowers, birds, candles, holiday lights, and dipa lamps (tiny clay oil lamps).

Craft Tissue Dipa Lamps

Copy and cut out oaktag dipa lamp patterns (page 86). Tear and glue craft tissue to the lamp form. Trim excess craft tissue when the glue has dried. Cut three different-sized circles, one each from yellow, orange, and white craft tissue. Glue the circles and dipa lamp to a dark sheet of construction paper. Cut a bright yellow craft tissue flame and attach it to the lamp. You can substitute gift wrap for craft tissue to decorate your dipa lamp.

Christmas

Christmas occurs on December 25. People all over the world decorate, prepare special foods, and spend time with their families. Many celebrations include singing and exchanging gifts.

Jingle Bell Gloves

Each child will need a pair of old gloves, a needle and thread, 10 jingle bells, scissors, glue, yarn scraps, sequins, buttons, and bows. Help children sew one bell to the end of each finger on both gloves. Have them decorate the gloves with the crafts supplies listed here.

Hanukkah

Hanukkah, also known as the Jewish Festival of Lights, usually occurs during the month of December and lasts for eight days. During this holiday families exchange gifts and follow the tradition of lighting eight candles on a candelabra called a *menorah*, one on each night of the eight-day celebration.

Jar Lid Menorah

You will need baby food jar lids, nine votive candles, permanent markers, aluminum foil, craft glue, and a sturdy sheet of cardboard. Measure and cut the cardboard to hold nine stacks of jar lids. Cover the board and each jar lid with aluminum foil. Decorate the sides of each lid with permanent markers. Glue the lids together to form nine stacks. Then glue the stacks side by side on the foil-covered board. When the glue has dried, place a votive candle on each stack. (Note: This is a decorative menorah and not intended for use.)

Kwanzaa

On December 26, African American families celebrate *Kwanzaa*. During this seven-day celebration families emphasize the unity of family, exchange gifts, and light a candelabra with seven candles called a *kinara*. Each candle represents one of the seven principles of Kwanzaa: unity, self-determination, work and responsibility, cooperative economics, purpose, creativity, and faith.

Giant Kinaras

You will need seven paper towel tubes, yellow craft tissue, colored chalk, a narrow sheet of sturdy cardboard, scissors, glue, and red, black, and green construction paper. Cover the cardboard with a sheet of black construction paper. Then cover three paper towel tubes with red construction paper, three more with green, and the last tube with black construction paper. Decorate the tubes with chalk designs. Apply glue to one end of each tube and attach tubes side by side to the covered cardboard. Cut seven yellow craft tissue squares for flames. Leaving the black tube for last, each day stuff a flame in the top of one of the tubes.

Mardi Gras

Mardi Gras takes place on a Tuesday before Easter. Each year the carnival season, which begins in early January, ends on Mardi Gras day with a parade of floats and marching bands. Its origin dates back to an ancient Roman custom of merrymaking before a fast.

Marvelous Mardi Gras Masks and Maracas

Provide children with oaktag copies of the Mardi Gras patterns on page 87, two paper plates each, crayons, markers, a stapler, scissors, glue, yarn, and ribbon to make masks and noisemakers. Have children color and cut out the design patterns to glue onto their masks and the bottom of two paper plates. Cut out the eye holes and attach two yarn ties to the sides of each child's mask. Pour a small amount of rice on one of each child's paper plates. Then help children staple their plates together to form a noisemaker.

Martin Luther King Day

Martin Luther King, Jr., was an African American civil rights leader. He was also a minister, and received the Nobel Peace Prize in 1964. In 1983 a law was passed making the third Monday in January a legal public holiday in honor of the birth of Mr. King. Mr. King worked to bring people from all cultures together in peace.

Take My Hand Garland

Using a variety of flesh-tone paper, make several copies of the hand patterns on page 88. Provide children with crayons, markers, a hole punch, a pair of hands, and ribbon. Help children tie their hand patterns together with ribbon as shown. Staple each pair of hands together at the finger tips to form a garland. Hang the garland across the top of a door jamb or window.

Dragon Pattern

Dipa Lamp Pattern

Mardi Gras Designs and Mask

Hand Patterns

Flower Patterns

Easter

Easter is an important religious holiday that falls on a Sunday between March 22 and April 25. There are many Easter symbols. One is the egg, which represents new life.

Glitter Egg Garden

Reproduce a poster board egg (page 91) for each child. Provide crayons and scissors for children to color and cut out their eggs. Help each child use a brush to paint a thin layer of glue and sprinkle glitter on his or her egg. When the glue has dried, staple each egg to a paint stirrer. Display eggs on a display board covered with light blue paper and green construction paper grass.

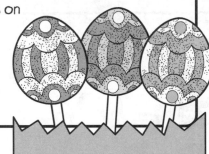

Mother's Day

Mother's Day was first celebrated in 1887. In 1904, Anna Jarvis of Philadelphia began the custom of wearing a carnation on the second Sunday in May. Then, in 1915, President Woodrow Wilson proclaimed Mother's Day a national celebration.

Mom Plaque

Reproduce the Mom plaque pattern on page 92 for each child. Provide crayons, markers, and scissors for children to color and cut out their pattern. Help each child punch two holes at the top of his or her plaque. Then attach a length of yarn for hanging.

Cinco de Mayo

On May 5, Mexicans celebrate the anniversary of their victory over French rule. Parades and celebrations continue into the night.

Pipe Cleaner Mosaic Flag

Reproduce a flag (page 90) on poster board for each child. Prepare three bowls filled with green, white, and red pipe cleaners cut to fit within the lines on the flag pattern. Have children color the center of their flags. Then have them glue on pipe cleaners to make stripes on their flags. Provide scissors to trim pipe cleaners if needed.

Celebrate Cinco de Mayo

May Day

On May Day many people celebrate the return of spring and new life. People sing, dance around maypoles, participate in festivals, and gather spring flowers to decorate for the celebration.

Coffee Can Flower Drum

Each child will need one large coffee can, two lids, construction paper, crayons, scissors, glue, markers, a wooden dowel, ribbon, and several copies of the flower patterns on page 88. Prepare coffee cans before you begin this project by cutting open the remaining end and using sandpaper to file the edges. Help children measure, cut, color, and glue construction paper and flowers around their cans. Then attach the lids to the top and bottom of the cans. Have children decorate wooden dowels with markers. Cut a few lengths of ribbon to glue to one end of each child's dowel.

Mosaic Flag Pattern

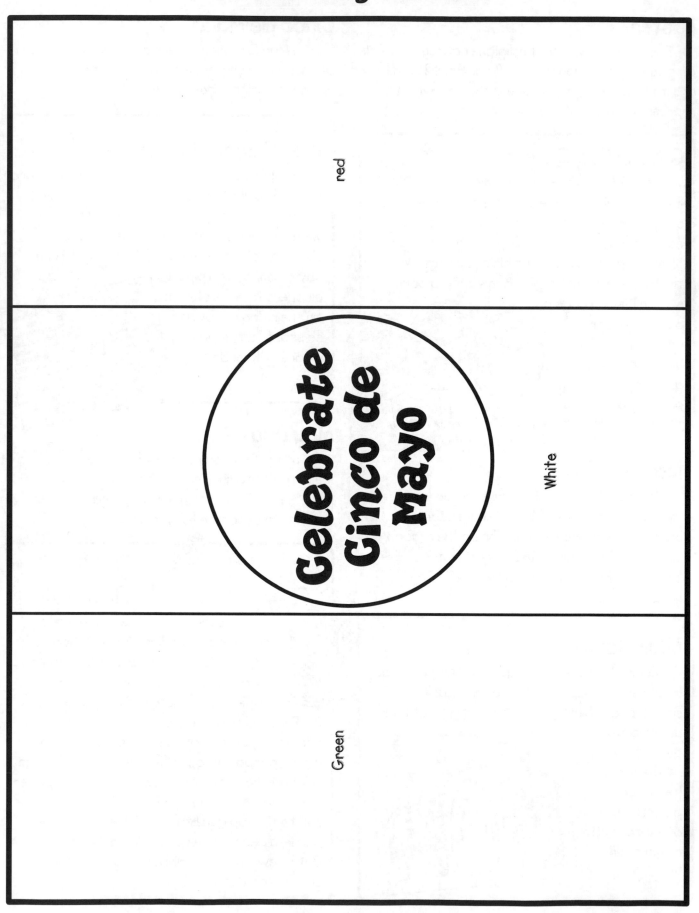

red

Celebrate Cinco de Mayo

White

Green

Egg Pattern

Mom Plaque Pattern

Passover

Passover is the Jewish festival of freedom. During Passover, which occurs during mid-spring, Jewish families celebrate at a feast called a *Seder*. During the celebration, the head of the family reads the story of Passover aloud.

Pasta Star Mosaic

Provide each child with aluminum foil, a variety of pasta noodles, scissors, glue, and a poster board star pattern (this page). Have children cut out and cover their stars with aluminum foil. Then have them glue pasta noodles on their stars.

Saint Patrick's Day

On March 17, Saint Patrick's Day is celebrated in honor of the patron saint of Ireland. Parades are held in many cities and people wear green clothing, shamrocks, and flowers.

Glitter Bug Shamrocks

Provide each child with a green pompon, wiggle eyes, pipe cleaners, yarn, scissors, glitter, glue, a brush, a shamrock pattern (this page), and a safety pin. Have children paint on glue, sprinkle glitter, and cut out their shamrocks. Then help each child cut and glue six yarn legs, two pipe cleaner antennae, and two wiggle eyes to his or her pompon. Have children sprinkle on glitter and glue the pompon bug on the shamrock. Tape a safety pin to the back of each shamrock to make glittery pins.

Star Pattern

Shamrock Pattern

Canada Day

Canada Day is one of Canada's most important national holidays. On July 1, the people of Canada celebrate the anniversary of the day when all the Canadian provinces became united under one government.

Maple Leaf Sponge Art

Cover a workstation with newspaper, then add shallow containers filled with red tempera paint, sponges cut into small pieces, and white construction paper. Make several maple leaf (page 95) oaktag stencils to place at the workstation. Have children put on smocks. Then have them sponge-paint their sheets of paper. When the paint has dried, help each child trace and cut out a maple leaf from their sponged paper. Mount leaves on a "Celebrate Canada Day" display board.

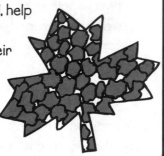

Father's Day

Father's Day comes each year on the third Sunday in June. Many people give their father gifts and greeting cards as an expression of love and gratitude.

Eyedropper Bow Ties

Cover a workstation with newspaper, then add margarine tubs filled with diluted food coloring, and eyedroppers. Then copy the bow tie on page 95 onto a paper towel for each child. Have children put on smocks. Demonstrate how to use an eyedropper to decorate a paper towel bow tie. Have children decorate their bow ties. While bow ties are drying, have each child draw a picture of his or her father on a sheet large sheet of construction paper. Help children write a Father's Day message and cut out a bow tie to attach to each portrait.

Happy Father's Day

Flag Day

Families, businesses, and public buildings display American flags on June 14 to celebrate the anniversary of the day the Continental Congress adopted the stars and stripes as the official flag of the United States.

Fringed Foil Flags

Provide aluminum foil, permanent markers, tape, scissors, and plastic straws for children to make fringed flags. Help each child cut an aluminum foil rectangle and cut fringe along all four edges. Then have children draw on stars and stripes and tape on a straw.

Independence Day

On July 4, Americans celebrate the anniversary of their independence from British rule. On this day, cities across the United States celebrate at picnics, attend parades, play games, and end the day with a fireworks display.

The Colors of Independence

Provide each child with a copy of the patterns on page 96, crayons or markers, and scissors. Help each child cut out and tape his or her patterns to form the word Independence. Then have children decorate their signs using colors that make them think of celebrating freedom.

Maple Leaf Pattern

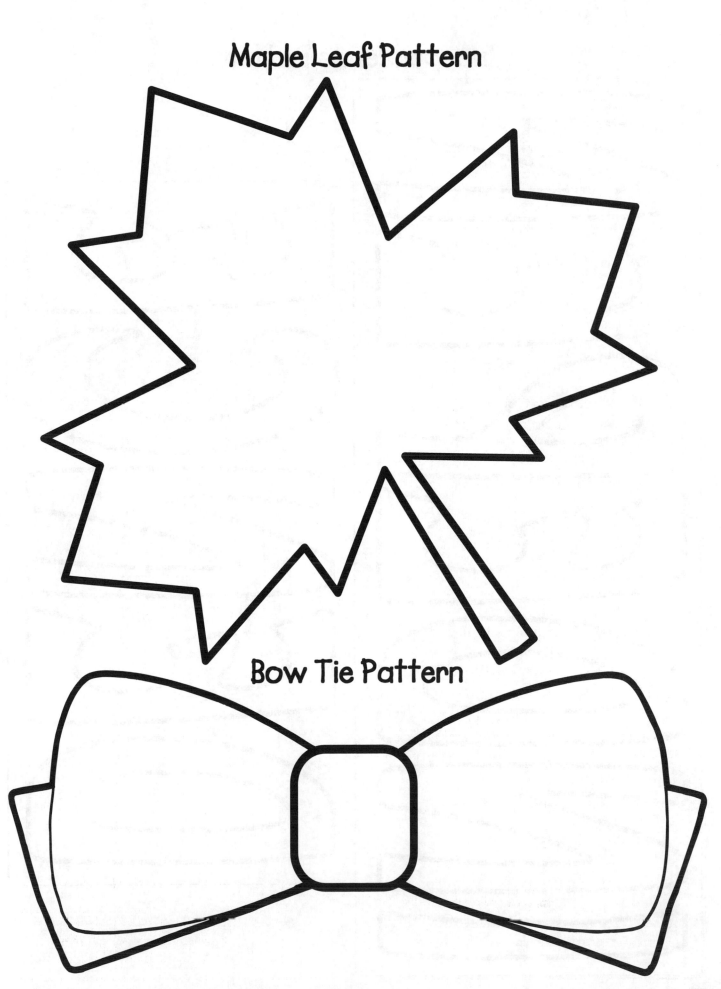

Bow Tie Pattern

Independence Pattern